A JOURNEY THROUGH LIFE AND HISTORY

INDIGORIVER
PUBLISHING

A JOURNEY THROUGH LIFE AND HISTORY

An Autobiographical Sketch

RADOMYSL TWARDOWSKI

Library of Congress Control Number: 2024914914

ISBN: 978-1-964686-09-7 (paperback)   978-1-964686-10-3 (ebook)

This book is based on true events reflecting the author's memory of them. Some names and characteristics may have been changed, some events compressed, and some dialogue recreated.

Editors: Dianna Graveman, Noëlla Simmons
Cover and Interior Design: Emma Elzinga

Printed in the United States of America

First Edition

3 West Garden Street, Ste. 718
Pensacola, FL 32502
www.indigoriverpublishing.com

Ordering Information:

Quantity sales: Special discounts are available on quantity purchases by corporations, associations, and others. For details, contact the publisher at the address above.

Orders by US trade bookstores and wholesalers: Please contact the publisher at the address above.

With Indigo River Publishing, you can always expect great books, strong voices, and meaningful messages. Most importantly, you'll always find . . . *words worth reading.*

A JOURNEY THROUGH LIFE AND HISTORY

PREFACE

As I look back at my life so far, I am filled with gratitude for all the events that led me to this point. I recall the people I met or gathered around me, walked alongside, and later lost. I remember the schools I attended, the plans either made and fulfilled or corrected and abandoned. I take stock of everything and ask myself: What was the driving force behind all of this? As we go through life, our self-understanding grows. We look for truth, for freedom, for love. Life is about becoming what our Creator intended for us to become. It is looking inside, at what we may call our inner conscience, our heart of hearts, and our soul. It is striving to apply the transcendent words of Our Lord in the Gospel of Matthew 11:29: "Take My yoke upon you and learn from Me."

This book is about sharing the message of faith, seeking truth and true health, and finding happiness and freedom. It is about overcoming our own weaknesses, doubts, and mistakes; external obstacles; and setbacks. We must go forward with gratitude, engaging our will and looking inside our heart and soul, because that is where we can find the voice of God, His forgiveness, and peace.

May 13, 2024
Feast of Our Lady of Fatima

Chapter 1

THE EARLY YEARS

1.

I entered the world on December 8, 1959, in Kraków, Poland.
My parents, Zbylut and Halina nee Nowosielska, were living with Mother's parents, Karol, and Eugenia, and working in the medical field after completing their studies in 1958. Mother's two younger sisters, Joanna and Barbara (Basia), lived there, too. Father's parents, Józef and Marianna, lived in Chorzów, sixty miles (ninety kilometers) due west, in the region of Upper Silesia, close to the prewar Polish-German border. Baptism took place on February 21, 1960, in St. Nicholas Church, also on Kopernika Street. Kraków is a historical city of churches and monuments; it can stimulate one's imagination along with an appreciation for history, inviting us to look at life as a continuous unfolding over which we do not possess full control but, in fact, have only a small part in the big drama.

The first four years in Kraków went by for me quickly. I have only traces of memories of early walks in the city to the Market Square (Rynek), to the city park encircling the Old Town (Planty), and to St. Nicholas Church or the Jesuit Church on Kopernika Street. The first trip to Wawel Cathedral happened around that time.

On later trips, around the age of eight or ten years, the solemn grandeur and religious atmosphere of the place started to have an impact on me. It became clear to me that Poland's history was rooted in Christianity. Grandfather Karol was always the guide. We usually approached Wawel Hill from the east, from Stradomska Street, and took a steep walkway to the Castle Courtyard. We would pass a large equestrian monument of General Tadeusz Kościuszko, a hero of the Polish Uprising of 1794, and earlier, of the American Revolutionary War that took place in 1775–1783.

The large bone of a prehistoric animal greeted us at the entrance to the main chapel. Almost immediately after entering, we faced the tombs of King Władysław Jagiełło on the left and the symbolic empty tomb (cenotap) of his son Władysław Warneńczyk on the right. A golden coffin with the relics of St. Stanisław of Szczepanów stood in the middle nave, leading to the main altar area.

My younger brother, Przemysław, was born in July 1963. The family moved to Bytom in November that year. I remember the moment I welcomed Przemek when Mother and a nurse walked out of the maternity ward with the nurse carrying him in her arms. He was sleeping calmly and had shapely features. I was happy but also twinges of anxiety and jealousy surfaced that I would no longer be the only apple of my mother's eye.

Bytom was ten miles northwest of Chorzów. In Bytom, Father became head of the department of nephrology at Szpital Górniczy, which served miners. He treated chronic kidney problems, using a dialysis machine, and developed new methods, catheters, formulas, and clinical approaches during his long, academically oriented career. Mother started working in the psychiatry department at the same hospital.

In Bytom, the family received the keys to the apartment in the building owned by and located close to Szpital Górniczy. Our apartment was initially on the fourth floor. Unfortunately, the water pressure was low, and sometimes running water was available only at night. There was no elevator, and mother had to carry her younger son, and frequently other items, up the stairs. Mom struggled physically at times, and although I tried to help, it likely had limited effect since I was still small.

In November 1963, the tragic news of the assassination of President Kennedy quickly reached the entire world. A new East German-made, black-and-white "Stadion" TV that stood in our apartment delivered the evening news that day. My mother responded with sadness and horror.

A year later, the same TV allowed us to receive a broadcast of the Games of the XVIII Olympiad from Tokyo. I was captivated by two track and field events with the US sprinters Henry Carr and Michael Larrabee winning men's 200 m and 400 m, respectively. In the latter race, Poland's Andrzej Badeński won the bronze. Watching the competition gave me an appreciation for the sport of track and field. I gathered knowledge of the events, results, and names of the leading athletes, including winners of the Olympic and European Championship medals. (Athletics World Championships started in 1983. The first edition was staged in Helsinki, Finland, and in 1991 became a biennial event.) My interest in the sport provided many hours of private enjoyment and prompted lively discussions among family members and friends.

Preschool and kindergarten started at that time, and it was fun after I got over my initial apprehension. I made a scene once on the street, dug in my heels, and very reluctantly entered the building after being forcibly persuaded by my mother and another adult.

Although I don't recall the names of my kindergarten friends, I remember a field trip to the theater to watch the play *Zimowe Przejazdki* ("Winter Rides"). I also remember learning to pronounce and understand new words. The kindergarten levels were called *maluszki* ("little babies"), *maluchy* ("bigger babies"), *średniaki* ("juniors"), and *starszaki* ("seniors"); at the senior level we read letters and words from the first ABC book. I joined the program at the maluchy level in the fall of 1963 and graduated in June 1966.

Despite living in Bytom, we returned to Kraków for every major holiday, including Easter, All Saints Day (November 1), and Christmas. It was always a precious time with Grandfather Karol, who asked us to call him by his nickname, *Lolek*; my grandmother Eugenia or *Gena*; and my maternal aunts, Joanna and Basia.

We kept close contact with the family in Edinburgh, Scotland. Grandfather's youngest brother, Włodzimierz (Włodek), an engineer by training and an accomplished chess player, found himself in Britain with the Polish Army during World War II. He decided to stay there and married a Scottish woman named Grace. They had four children: Alexandra (Oleńka), Barbara, Anna, and Charles (Charlie). They visited Kraków several times, traveling in Uncle Włodek's Vauxhall Victor, a car that was a class above the average Polish, East German, or Czechoslovakian car such as Syrena, Warszawa, Trabant, Wartburg, Skoda Octavia, or Skoda 1000 MB.

Unfortunately, Uncle Włodek passed away in Edinburgh in 1965, shortly after his vacation in Poland. He had heart trouble, which started at the end of the vacation and bothered him on the return journey.

Grandmother Gena had five brothers and hosted pleasant gatherings at Christmas. In Poland, December 26 (the official Second Day of Christmas and a state holiday even in the communist system) was always devoted to family visits. Grandmother's youngest brother Mieczysław (Mietek) turned one hundred in November 2022, an achievement that was celebrated with warm appreciation in the family. Grandfather Lolek had two brothers in Poland and two brothers who emigrated.

Elementary school always started on September 1, unless it fell on a Sunday. The school year always ended on or around June 20.

The year I turned seven—1966—was a special year in Poland's history. We celebrated a thousand years of the Polish state. (In 966 AD, Prince Mieszko I had been baptized on Holy Saturday, April 14.)

As first graders, we were too young to grasp the political nuances of history. Only in later years were we able to understand what had transpired. There was a political competition between the Communist state (Poland was officially atheistic and under the tutelage of USSR since 1947) and the Catholic Church, which remained popular and powerful. Communists, led by the first secretary of the Polish United Workers' Party (Communist party), Władysław Gomułka, emphasized the secular aspect of the establishment of Poland. However, the Church in the 1960s, led by Cardinal Stefan Wyszyński, was truly "of the people" and had more grounding in the nation than the Communist party in terms of the numbers and the depth and authenticity of convictions. Later, as everywhere in the world, the Church was infiltrated by hostile elements, and clear distinctions between good and evil became blurred.

There was a strict separation of church and state at that time. Religious themes were not discussed in school, but every parish church provided religious education. Under my first Catechist, Fr. Zbigniew Stępkowski, I studied the Old and the New Testaments, the Ten Commandments, and the Catechism. I liked attending religion classes, which took place in the evening. I felt very much at home with the curriculum, but as was the case with sports, I did not feel called to become a lay theologian or Church historian. Medical tradition was strong in my family.

After class one day in about 1970, a boy in a group of five or six snuck up on me. I do not know his motives; likely he did not fancy my diligence in class very much. I ran away from the unfriendly group, but they pursued me and gave me two or three blows to the face before I made it to the apartment less than half a mile away.

I usually tried to stay away from trouble in school, but there were fisticuffs on four or five occasions. I knew immediately that boxing or MMA was not going to be my thing and that I should learn to control my emotions much better in the future.

In 1967 I attended second grade in Kraków for three or four months while Mother had her specialization course in psychiatry at the Jagiellonian Medical College.

I also started additional tutoring in English that year from a high school teacher in Bytom. It provided a good background for subsequently learning the language upon coming to America in 1983. My brother did the same four years later.

I once memorized a quote (in English, of course) from Baron Pierre de Coubertin, the second president of the International Olympic Committee: "The most important thing in the Olympic Games is not to win but to take part, just as the most important thing in life is not the triumph but the struggle. The essential thing is not to have conquered but to have fought well." The teacher, Ms. Irena, and my fellow student, Jacek, nodded in appreciation.

In the meantime, we also moved that year from the fourth-floor apartment to the second-floor apartment, which was more convenient to access, especially for my mother with shopping bags and a baby carriage for my younger brother. The issues with low water pressure also improved.

The following year, 1968, was another momentous year for Poland. We were still too young in the second and third grade to grasp the details of the politics but sensed that something was "wrong" in the country. In March there were strikes mostly at the academic centers against the policies of the Polish United Workers' Party. There was a reaction from the security forces, Urzad Bezpieczenstwa (UB), to suppress the strikes and subsequently the entire dissident movement. Simultaneously, there began an "anti-Zionist" campaign, which was a result of the power struggle within the party and resulted in forced emigration of at least 13,000 Poles of Jewish origin whom the government fired from their positions and subjected to other forms of harassment.

I received the First Holy Communion at the Holy Cross Church in Bytom in May, and I was provided short pants to wear for the occasion, which disappointed me. Maybe it was a matter of cost and the financial situation was temporarily difficult at that time; maybe there were other reasons. I offered this pain to God whom I was receiving.

That year was also very turbulent in the United States. In January there was an escalation of the Vietnam War in the form of Tet Offensive, which ended with the South Vietnamese/US victory but at the cost of civilian casualties. The US public opinion had turned against the war. Dr. Martin Luther King Jr. and Sen. Robert F. Kennedy were assassinated, and incumbent president, Lyndon Baines Johnson, did not seek reelection. There were riots at the Democratic Party convention in Chicago. Richard M. Nixon was elected the thirty-seventh US president, defeating the incumbent vice-president, Hubert Humphrey.

The games of the XIX Olympiad took place in Mexico City in October against this political backdrop and were additionally preceded by the demonstrations calling for greater civil and democratic rights.

There were political demonstrations during the Olympics by the athletes, most notably by Tommie Smith and John Carlos, gold and bronze medalists in the 200-meter race. Wearing only human rights badges and black socks, the men lowered their heads and raised black-gloved fists in solidarity with the Black Freedom Movement in the United States as the "Star-Spangled Banner" played.

Of note is that the United States won the overall medal count with forty-five golds, twenty-eight silvers, and thirty-four bronzes. The Soviet Union turned in a subpar, by their standards, performance with twenty-nine golds, thirty-two silvers, and thirty bronzes, which was more than sufficient for second place. Traditionally strong teams of Japan, Hungary, East Germany, and France finished next, with Czechoslovakia in seventh place, which was one of their best showings in history. Poland was in eleventh place with five golds, two silvers, and eleven bronzes. This was the only time Poland finished out of the top ten between 1960 and 1980.

In July 1969 my family vacationed in Chałupy, in Hel Peninsula, north of Gdańsk, on the Baltic Sea, as we did every July from 1964 to 1980. The only exceptions were in 1971 and 1972 when we went to Lake Balaton in Hungary, and in 1975 and 1976 when Mother received an opportunity for further specialization in psychiatry at Leicester General Hospital in England. Also in 1976, Father flew to America in June to work in Columbia, Missouri, as a nephrology fellow at University Hospital for a year, sharing his experiences from the celebrations of America's Bicentennial with us in letters and brief phone conversations. I went to the Pojezierze Mazurskie (Warmia-Masuria Lake District) in 1975 and 1976, but in 1977 we all made it back to Chałupy again in full force.

The first half of July 1969 was marked by the sad event of Grandfather Karol's brother passing. Uncle Adolf (Dolek) returned from America and reached the city of Poznań via Berlin. His heart could not manage the great emotion of the moment. Mother interrupted her vacation and attended the funeral in Kraków.

Later in July, the first moon landing occurred, and the Apollo 11 crew of Neil Armstrong, Edwin Aldrin, and Michael Collins became household names in Poland. For some reason Władysław Gomułka allowed the live transmission to take place, which was not the case in other Eastern Bloc countries. He wanted to show that Poland was trying to keep up with the latest developments in the West and was not an ossified, anti-Western society. The party did not allow Paul VI[1] to visit Poland for the Millennium of Christianity in 1966, and a hardline nationalistic campaign had taken place in the major academic centers in Poland just a year earlier.

In 1970 modernity had been advancing fast, even in the Soviet Bloc, with electronic equipment, automobiles, new foods, clothes, and dress fashions multiplying in stores and in people's homes. In June the Ninth FIFA World Cup (Copa Mundial de Futbol), was played in Mexico, and with the advancements in satellite communications, the finals attracted a new record television audience as games were broadcast live around the world. We had a chance to go to Szczyrk (a ski resort in southern Poland, close to the Czechoslovak border) to watch the last four games of the finals. The signals were "mooched" from the television transmitter in Ostrava, Czechoslovakia, because Gomułka this time did not agree

---

1   The Sedevacantist position holds that all the claimants to the papal throne since October 28, 1958, were not truly Catholic, hence, they were not true popes. Therefore, their promulgations and actions do not represent authentic Catholic Magisterium but a deception and an anti-Church. The author's own conviction on this subject has become much clearer and stronger since writing this book, and he would like to return to it in future writings.

to buy broadcasting rights from TVP, a move for which he was roundly criticized and which contributed to his losing the position as de facto Poland's political leader six months later. Our guess was that Gomułka wanted to set the brakes on the liberalization process and also wanted to save money to balance the budget for the fiscal year. He was frugal, even miserly, as the population perceived him. Poland was not in the finals anyway.

For the record, the great Brazil team won the World Cup with the help of their stars, led by Pele. Italy, Germany, and Uruguay also had teams of sublime quality, but Brazil's winning eleven in 1970 is still considered by the experts as the best team in history.

At the end of the year, massive protests occurred in Gdańsk and other cities, caused by sudden increases in the prices of basic foods. The protests lasted from December 14 through 19 and were suppressed by the army and militia. At least forty-four people were killed, and more than a thousand wounded. Since there were no free elections at that time, periodic crises, protests, and riots were the only unhappy occasions to change the government leadership. And so it happened that Gomułka (in power since 1956) was replaced by Edward Gierek who, as a former miner and worker himself, promised transparency and wage increases, and to rule "with" the workers, not against them.

2.

In February 1971 we went to Szczyrk again, this time during school winter break to ski for a week. Connections had been established previously with the property owners to rent a mountainside room in a solid brick house with good accommodation. The slope side conditions were spartan, there were very few lifts in the area we chose to ski, and every yard of elevation had to be gained by climbing the mountain with or without the skis attached to the boots. The equipment was rented in town, and there was not enough time to become familiar with it.

That fateful morning, nothing came easy. I slipped and slid while climbing the mountain. The skis kept coming off, so I tightened the bindings. After gaining altitude, I decided to ski down the slope and, as if to compensate for the previous struggle, be more daring. I attempted parallel turns (Kristiania, the term coming from Norway, called "a cradle of skiing") instead of the more conservative "wedge turn" or "plough." Unfortunately, in deep powder the left ski did not turn when my knee had already made its 90-degree twist. The binding was set too tight, the ski did not come loose, and I felt sharp pain and heard a sharp rasping sound in my knee. Naturally, I fell, grinding my teeth, shedding tears of pain and frustration. My vacation was over, and I would have a long recovery ahead.

We got back to Bytom in two to three days and an orthopedic doctor examined me. This was a renowned specialist, Dr. Janusz Daab, from a family of German roots, well known in the region of Silesia. There was no computer tomography (CT) or magnetic resonance imaging (MRI) yet, but I had X-rays, followed by a needle drainage of the knee, which accumulated blood. Fortunately, the ligaments were only sprained, not torn. I rehabbed the knee and returned to normal life, although I felt that the knee could not bear full weight at times, especially during the toe-off phase of a gait or run; it certainly affected endurance running, soccer, and track. Many years later, in December 2016, Dr. Christopher Robertson in Fargo, North Dakota performed a meniscectomy and chondroplasty, which dramatically improved the situation. I was able to engage in a sustained recreational running program, having completed 5K, 10K, and half-marathon runs, as well as one full marathon in Fargo in 2018. I am grateful for the great surgeons I met who guided my knee to recovery. I thought of the athletes engaged in high-level competition and sustained worse injuries, struggling to return to full training. There was a soccer star player, Włodzimierz Lubański, who injured his knee in June 1973 in a 2:0 victory over England a few minutes after scoring the second goal for Poland. He returned to playing in 1976, unable to achieve his previous prowess but still able to make important contributions to the national team until retiring in 1980. Orthopedic surgery, along with other medical specialties, has made tremendous progress since that time.

During this entire time, school was especially important. It was my primary preoccupation, and I tried to get good grades. Polish language, history, geography, and biology came easier than math and physics, but I was trying to become well-rounded.

I received the Sacrament of Confirmation in May 1971. My Confirmation sponsor was Jerzy, a son of Grandmother Gena's brother, Uncle Wojciech. The bishop who administered the Sacrament to me and other fifth graders at the Church of the Holy Cross was Monsignor Franciszek Jop, who was the Apostolic Administrator in Opole, sixty miles (one hundred kilometers) northwest of Bytom. The Diocese of Opole was not formally erected until June 1972 (from a part of the Diocese of Wrocław, formerly Breslau), after a period of transition between the German administration and Polish administration when the borders moved westwards after World War II ended in 1945. Bytom still belonged to the Diocese of Katowice in 1971, where Monsignor Herbert Bednorz had been a bishop since 1967. Due to many Confirmations, the bishops' schedule was busy, and the prelates had to help each other. In 1992 Bytom emerged in the newly formed Diocese of Gliwice.

In July, Barbara (Basia), Mother's youngest sister, married Aleksander (Olek) Mitka, at the Church of St. Nicholas. He worked as an art restorer; it was their family tradition. The wedding reception was quite sumptuous. It took place at a large family home in Januszowice, six miles (ten kilometers) north of Kraków. I remember a brief ride in a BMW 1602 two-door coupe with Basia's friend; my brother and I were passengers in the back. We talked to many people, ran around the property, listened to music, and even played soccer ball, which completed the trajectory after my kick and hit an elderly gentleman on the side of the face. He was dazed for a moment, and I pretended I did not know what had happened. A few months later, someone tossed a brick into the yard in front of our apartment building in Bytom and hit me in the left temple. I heard a loud buzz in my head for a long time afterwards; I "saw stars" and staggered, although I did not lose consciousness. I now have a 40 percent hearing loss in my left ear, which may be related to that event.

As mentioned before, we went to Czechoslovakia and Hungary in July 1971 and 1972. It was a pleasant experience. Both countries appeared a bit tidier and economically better developed than Poland. Budapest and Prague were magnificent, historic cities. Matthias Church, the Fisherman's Bastion in Buda, and the Island of Margaret on the Danube River, which had thermal spas with artificial waves, were memorable. There were cafes with ice cream and widely available Coca-Cola, which the company introduced in Poland barely a year later. Prague had its Old City, St. Vitus Cathedral, and Charles Bridge. At that time, these monuments may have had a more "authentic" feel about them as a bastion of opposition to Communism rather than as merely a tourist attraction in an increasingly secular society after the fall of Communism. We wondered about the attitudes of Czechs and Slovaks toward the tourists from beyond their northern border, knowing the Warsaw Pact troops had invaded their country just three years earlier, but everything was incredibly positive.

After I finished sixth grade in 1972, there was a school reorganization, and we moved from the Jan Smoleń School Number 50 on Strzelców Bytomskich (Bytom's Riflemen) Street to School Number 12 on the street named after the thirty-second US president, Franklin Delano Roosevelt. Students completed the seventh and eighth grades there; ninth grade and high school were held in the building that had previously housed School Number 50, now renamed Smoleń Liceum.

The years 1972 and 1973 were interesting, optimistic, and marked by economic growth in Poland. We had more money in our wallets and could buy more clothes, including such Western brands as Levi's and Wrangler jeans. Edward Gierek, trying to be true to his promise of good administration, obtained $40 billion worth of loans and credits from the

West and started building industrial projects and roads, and developing manufacturing plants. There were technological advancements, including articles of daily use. Poland started mass production of automobiles based on the Italian FIAT technology.

The XX Olympic Games took place in Munich from August 26 to September 11, another athletic spectacle of the highest quality. Since the Federal Republic of Germany was near Poland, there was no time difference, and we could watch the events in prime time. Polish TV allocated many hours of the programming to broadcast track and field, soccer, gymnastics, and swimming. Mark Spitz of the US was the great performer, winning seven gold medals with seven world records in swimming. Olga Korbut, a Byelorussian gymnast representing Soviet Union, won three golds and a silver. Poland's Władysław Komar won the men's shot put by the smallest of margins (1cm) over the favorite George Woods of the US. Poland won the Olympic soccer competition, defeating Hungary 2:1 in the final. The Soviet Union won the most gold medals and overall medals. The United States was in the second place.

There was a terrorist attack by eight members of the Palestinian militant organization Black September on September 5. The group infiltrated the Olympic Village. It was another chapter in the ongoing saga of the Israeli-Palestinian conflict, which always tends to produce retaliatory measures. Seventeen people died: twelve victims (hostages) and five perpetrators.

In the seventh and eighth grades, I focused increasingly on the study of biology and chemistry in preparation for my future: the study of medicine. I also continued my interest in humanities, journalism, history, and current events. As chief editor of our school's biweekly newspaper, *Agora* (Greek for the Latin word *forum*), I did my best to help broaden horizons and be of service to my fellow students.

In October 1973, the editorial board of Agora, comprised of four people (three coeditors and me), had the privilege to visit a noted author of youth literature, Alfred Szklarski. We were able to interview him in

Katowice, the capital of the Silesia region, and publish the material in our school newspaper. Our Polish literature teacher, Ms. Krystyna Kojder, was the inspiration for and a facilitator of the entire Agora enterprise and of this special interview. Mr. Szklarski's most famous work is a nine-book series of adventure novels about Tomek Wilmowski and a group of friends, including his father. The group left Poland in the beginning of the twentieth century when Poland fell under Russian occupation. They went on to visit all the continents starting from "the land of the kangaroos," then on to "the Black Continent" and then North America, where Tomek's friend Sally Allen is kidnapped. Later books take Tomek and friends to Central Asia, "tracing Yeti," then South America, Papua New Guinea, and again to South America at the source of the Amazon River and Gran Chaco. This series sparked our imaginations and awakened our senses to the world, even though foreign travel was not yet possible for most Poles at that time.

Seven days after our interview, on October 17, 1973, Poland finally gained entry to the next edition of the FIFA World Cup, which was planned for June and July 1974 in West Germany. It was Poland's second time ever, after its exciting debut in 1938 in which it had lost to Brazil 5:6. Leonidas was the star for Brazil, and Poland's Ernst Willimowski remains the only player in World Cup history to have scored four goals in a losing game. The game at Wembley Stadium was a shrewd, tactical affair ending in a 1:1 draw. Following the 2:0 victory four months earlier in Chorzów (and still only victory against England so far), during which Lubański was injured, his colleagues acquitted themselves well in London. Twenty-three-year-old Grzegorz Lato, who was a driving force behind the offensive actions of the team, goalkeeper Jan Tomaszewski, defender Jerzy Gorgoń, midfielder Kazimierz Deyna with his excellent vision, and left-winger Robert Gadocha were at the top of their form and were among the leading players in Europe at that time.

Another author who made an immense impression on me and my brother, and many people in our school circle, was Edmund Niziurski.

In his long life and career after World War II he wrote dynamic, witty, and humorous stories mostly revolving around the everyday school life of his teenage characters. I really immersed myself in the elaborate plots of such books as *Księga Urwisów* ("The Book of the Brats"), *Niewiarygodne Przygody Marka Piegusa* ("Unbelievable Adventures of Marek Piegus [Freckle]"), *Awantura w Niekłaju* ("A Row in Niekłaj"), and *Siódme Wtajemniczenie* ("The Seventh Initiation"). These books are set in the postwar period of the 1950s and 1960s and describe the drab realities of socialism and political facts of collectivization and nationalization of the economy, opposed by "the enemies of the people." But they included colorful action and language, humor, scenes of competition, conflicts and skirmishes among students, interactions between professors and students, kidnappings, and rescues, with a message of triumph, good over evil, and faith in the rationality of people's actions. These books enhanced the imagination and the vocabulary of young readers.

Two TV series in the late 1960s and early 1970s, *Stawka Większa niż Życie* ("Stakes Larger Than Life") and *Czterej Pancerni i Pies* ("Four Tank-Men and a Dog") were very popular and occupied our attention for an hour once a week.

Stawka was about the adventures of a Polish intelligence officer who acts as a double agent in the Abwehr between 1942 and 1945.

The tankmen and their dog *Szarik* (Ball) start their journey from the first battle of the Polish forces in the East at Lenino in the Mogylev region of Byelorussia on October 12, 1943, and end it in Berlin on May 9, 1945.

Both series brought human dimension to the war effort. The conflict revealed itself through the fates of the main characters showing their ingenuity and perseverance and reinforcing our feeling of Poland's role in World War II. Wartime events set between the steppes and forests of Russia, Byelorussia, and Ukraine, and the plains and cities of Poland and Germany, came to life, shown with suspense, precision and elan. Both series were in black and white, but this did not detract from their artistic impact. Above all, there was a gripping fictional plot with many subplots and impossible survival outcomes, bordering on comedic; it was great entertainment to which we returned with pleasure.

Also, a film adaptation of Henryk Sienkiewicz's historical novels *Pan Wołodyjowski* ("Colonel Wolodyjowski") in 1969 and *Potop* ("The Deluge") in 1974 made a huge artistic impact on me. They were filmed in the reverse order of their sequence in *The Trilogy*, written by Sienkiewicz from 1884 through 1887, commencing from "With Fire and Sword." ("With Fire and Sword" was filmed last, in 1999 after the fall of the Eastern Bloc, when previous Polish-Ukrainian conflicts of 1647–1648 could finally be discussed with more openness). "The Deluge" describes the adventures of a nobleman, Kmicic, around the time of the Swedish War in 1655. "Pan Wołodyjowski" is set against the backdrop of the Polish-Ottoman Wars of 1669–1683 with the main protagonist giving the title to the book and film (he also figures prominently in the first part of *The Trilogy*). There are moving romantic threads in each book. The characters Kloss and Brunner in *Stawka*; Janek, Gustlik, Olgierd, Tomek, and Grigory in "Tankmen"; and Michał Wołodyjowski, Jan Skrzetuski, Onufry Zagłoba, Longinus Podbipięta, and Andrzej Kmicic in *The Trilogy* became a part of the historical, popular, national-military lore, and the actors, linked to their characters, familiar faces on Poland's cultural scene.

I finished strong in the eighth grade. I studied biology, being interested in DNA, RNA, and the entire cell structure. I was fascinated with the history of ongoing discovery of DNA and RNA by James Watson, Francis Crick, and other scientists such as Rosalind Franklin, Linus Pauling, and Erwin Chargaff. I found the double helix of DNA to be an immensely elegant, well-programmed structure that carries out its functions of development, survival, and replication with supreme precision. (Swiss biologist Friedrich Miescher is credited with first isolating DNA in 1869). Likewise, I tried to become familiar with the species of plant and animal life. Algebra and geometry required more effort, but in a 5 (very good), 4 (good), 3 (sufficient), 2 (failing) grading system, I managed to have straight 5s on my elementary school certificate.

Chapter 2

HIGH SCHOOL

1.

The summer of 1974 was the most positive and heartwarming period in my life, the one to which I return with the fondest memories. The vacation schedule was busy, with a ten-day trek in the Beskidy Mountains in Southern Poland with a group of friends from school and the scout troop in Bytom. FIFA World Cup in West Germany started. Poland played very well; the team was even better than in 1973 and defeated Argentina 3:2, Haiti 7:0, and Italy 2:1 in the first round. (We were able to watch each game in a different hostel on our trip.) The second group stage I saw in Międzywodzie, on the Baltic seaside in northwestern Poland (pre-war Germany), on a camp of Bytom judo club. The name of the club was *Czarni* ("The Blacks," alluding to the coalmining industry in the Upper Silesia region). I was training judo for two years in 1973 and 1974 but realized it would not be my destiny; my left knee was weak at times, not giving full support to perform complicated throws. So, the camp in Międzywodzie was a "swan song." I told the trainer and manager about my decision to move on only after returning to Bytom. They were unhappy about it because I took the place of a better long-term prospect at the camp, although I gave my best effort in the allotted time. A pleasant memory is that the future two-time Olympic Champion (in 1988 and 1992) Waldemar Legień graced the section, and I can say that I trained with him for a while. He is almost four years younger than me (close to my brother's age), and we had little direct contact because of the height and weight difference at the time. But a photograph of the roster at the end of the camp features him and me among other colleagues in the same lineup.

After a day filled with training judo, we found time in the evenings to watch the exciting Soccer World Cup with Poland riding a high wave.

The second-round games were watched in the common room of our sports center; we were happy with the victories over Sweden 1:0, and Yugoslavia 2:1. A dramatic game on a very flooded pitch in Frankfurt resulted in a 0:1 loss against the hosts and eventual winners, West Germany. The third-place playoff brought another win, 1:0 against Brazil, the outgoing champions, after a solo run by Lato, which produced his seventh goal of the tournament, giving him the honor of a top scorer. Other strong players were Antoni Szymanowski, Władysław Żmuda, Adam Musiał in defense, Henryk Kasperczak, Zygmunt Maszczyk, Lesław Ćmikiewicz in midfield, and Andrzej Szarmach in the center of attack. Zmuda, Szarmach, and Lato would repeat a successful run for the bronze medal eight years later in Spain.

Kazimierz Górski was a head coach; he was an excellent psychologist and motivator, one of the noted coaches in history.

West Germany defeated Netherlands 2:1 in the final. We returned to Bytom soon thereafter.

2.

On Monday, September, I started ninth grade in high school. I chose a class with a biology-chemistry profile, meaning there were additional hours assigned for the study of these subjects over a general profile class.

There was also a class with the mathematics-physics profile.

I remember all our professors with gratitude. Our mathematics tutoress was Ms. Stankiewicz. Ms. Adamek taught English. Our biology teacher was Dr. Leopold Kobierski, a graduate student of Professor Władysław Szafer, who was a botanist, geologist, and world pioneer in nature conservation, and who served as rector of the Jagiellonian University from 1936 to 1938. Dr. Kobierski himself was an involved educator and ecologist. This area of study was important at that time in the region of Upper Silesia because the foul-smelling, visible gases and vapors from the coal mines and steel mills were truly a factor that negatively impacted the quality of air and life in general.

In the spring of 1975, there were field excursions to various nature reserve parks, most often to the Segiet forest around Bytom and Tarnowskie Góry. Dr. Kobierski, with his encyclopedic knowledge of various plants and insect species, encouraged us to collect them, memorize the names, and know their taxonomy and properties in a larger ecosystem. We went for a long weekend trip to Białowieża National Park, on the border of the Byelorussian Socialist Republic, a part of USSR. The forest was a treasure trove of rare and protected trees, ferns, and animals, including the European bison (żubr), reintroduced to the park in 1929, and saved from extinction.

Ninth grade went fast. I received a 5 in Polish, biology, history, and geography, and a 4 in mathematics and physics. Paternal Grandfather Józef died on June 29. He was a prisoner of a Nazi concentration camp during World War II and lived to be seventy-five, but in the last two to three years of life had been in poor health.

As previously mentioned, in the summer of 1975, I went to the northeastern region of the Warmia-Masuria Province with a group of fellow scouts from Bytom. The region was named East Prussia in the prewar period and belonged to Germany.

We undertook a bicycle trek and called it "Bicyklersi-75." A group of about twenty-five people took the train from Bytom and reached

Tczew. Our bicycle route started officially at the railway station in Tczew; then we rode to Malbork, fifteen miles eastward. There is a world-class tourist attraction in Malbork, a thirteenth-century Castle of the Teutonic Order. The largest castle in the world, with an area of 143,000 square meters (1,540,000 square feet), is an UNESCO World Heritage site. Eleven grand masters of the Teutonic Order from the fourteenth and fifteenth centuries are buried there.

The moat, the barbican, and the walls are immense. Inside, the great refectory with its columns and fan-vaulted ceilings reflects seven centuries of political, cultural, and religious meetings, banquets, treaties, and convocations. It is brought to life in the epic production of the Polish cinema *Krzyżacy* ("Teutonic Knights"), released in 1960, the 550th anniversary of the battle of Grunwald, which set the history of central-northern Europe for the following four hundred years. The film is based on Henryk Sienkiewicz's historical novel written in 1900, under the same title, for which and for other notable works, including *Quo Vadis* and the Trilogy, he was awarded the Nobel Prize in Literature in 1905.

The next stop was Frombork, 38 miles northeast of Malbork. It was a place of work, death, and burial of an astronomer, Nicolaus Copernicus (Mikołaj Kopernik). Born in 1473 in Toruń (Thorn, Royal Prussia, Kingdom of Poland), he studied at the universities in Kraków, then in Italy, and was engaged in notable scientific pursuits. His main claim to fame is the heliocentric model, which states the sun is in the center of the universe with the earth revolving around it. Kopernik worked as a Catholic canon in Frombork from 1522 to 1543, and his book *On the Revolutions of the Celestial Spheres* was published shortly before his death.

We rode eastward to Braniewo, Pieniężno, Lidzbark, Bisztynek, Reszel, and Święta Lipka (Holy Linden) with a beautiful church and moving pipe organ, possibly the finest church instrument ever constructed, reaching Kętrzyn (formerly Rastenburg) about twelve days later. This is called the Warmia region; the Masuria region extends further north and east. The final thrilling attraction of the trip was a visit to the site of Adolf Hitler's Eastern Front military headquarters at Gierłoż, five miles east of Kętrzyn, a fortress called "Wolf's Lair" (*Wilczy Szaniec* in Polish, *Wolfs Schanze* in German). Composed of eighty steel-reinforced concrete buildings, fifty of them bunkers, it was the site of a coup attempt against Hitler by bomb detonation, which failed and resulted in brutal reprisals by the fading and retreating German Reich. The leader of the plot was Colonel Claus von Stauffenberg, aptly portrayed by Tom Cruise in the movie *Valkyrie*, released in 2008.

After Gierłoż we reached Węgorzewo, then rode seventy to eighty kilometers (fifty to sixty miles) west to the regional capital Olsztyn and took the train back to Bytom.

3.

Tenth grade went well; I put more emphasis on the study of math and physics and managed to receive a 5 note from both. There were straight 5s without a single hour of study missed (I would repeat this score four years later during the second year of medical school). I felt happier in general, having started a friendship with a classmate named Teresa. She was a good student and a very pretty lady. I started to discover the meaning of friendship, the awareness of sexuality, and what it might entail to start a family in the future.

On October 2, 1975, we managed to get the tickets for the big soccer game between Poland and the Netherlands in EURO'76 qualifying stage. Other teams in "our" group were Italy and Finland. Poland played a great game, defeating the powerful Dutch team 4:1. Lato scored the first goal, then Gadocha and Szarmach (twice) stung the Dutch. In the dying moments, van de Kerkhof scored for the rivals. The encounter took place at the old Silesian Stadium (*Stadion Slaski*). A huge blue cloud of cigarette smoke hovered above the stadium before the game started. Only later, a non-smoking policy became the norm everywhere at similar events. Poland lost the return tie in Rotterdam 0:3 the next month, and the Dutch went into the last eight and then to the finals, which were staged in Yugoslavia for the last four teams. Czechoslovakia won the title, defeating West Germany in the final. The Netherlands finished third, and Yugoslavia was fourth.

A week after the end of the school year, in June 1976, there were protests in the Warsaw suburb of Ursus and in the city of Radom. They followed another attempted price increase by the government, which was falling into increasing debt. The protests were brutally pacified, and the price increase was shelved. Edward Gierek and Prime Minister Piotr Jaroszewicz looked economically foolish and politically weak. Gierek's long "honeymoon" was over, and the people felt that the country's economic progress had peaked and stalled, now heading toward a decline.

We went again to the Masurian Lake District in July on a kayak trip. The group had about twenty-two sophomores and juniors from our school and three to four older tutors. It was also organized under the auspices of the scout troop. We arrived in Olsztyn and then took the bus to Mikołajki, going through Mrągowo, having rented the canoes in Mikołajki. A beautiful waterway connects Mikołajki, Giżycko, and Węgorzewo, with lakes Śniardwy, Niegocin, Mamry, and other smaller ones strewn between the towns, an elaborate network of rivers and channels built since the eighteenth century. We ended up in the extreme northeast area of Poland in Augustów near Lake Wigry. Then we reached Suwałki near the Lithuanian border and took the train through Warsaw back to Bytom.

The kayaks were double; the crews were assigned to each other on a permanent basis, and I was obviously happy to form a team with Teresa. We liked each other and thought we might build a serious relationship. Evenings were organized around the scout campfires with the group singing patriotic and scout songs. One night I made my feelings toward Teresa known publicly by reciting by heart Sonnet 43: "How Do I Love Thee?" by Elizabeth Barrett Browning, with a masterly Polish translation by Ludmiła Marjańska. Teresa and the audience were impressed for a moment, but the magic of poetry did not seal our souls forever.

The XXI Olympic Games in Montreal took place in the second half of the month. We could not watch the events since we were sleeping in tents in the wild (as on a bike trip in the previous year), and there was a seven- or eight-hour time difference. We listened to the radio at times, learning about Irena Szewińska's victory in the women's 400 meter, gold medals by Jacek Wszoła in high jump (Greg Joy of Canada won the silver, and Dwight Stones of the United States the bronze), and Tadeusz Ślusarski in pole vault (Antti Kaliomaeki of Finland was second, and Dave Roberts of the United States was third). The gold in the men's 1600-meter race went to the US Team. Poland took the silver in that race, as did Bronisław Malinowski in 3000-meter steeplechase. We were impressed by the gold medal of Poland's volleyball team, which defeated the Soviet Union 3:2 in a nail-biting final. The handball team won the bronze medal. The soccer team lost to East Germany, 1:3, in the final. Soviet Union won the overall medal count and the United States came in third, this time also behind East Germany. Poland was in sixth place, highest ever in their Olympic history, trailing West Germany and Japan. The Montreal Games track and field competition is still close to my heart after all these years because of the high excitement generated and sportsmanship shown by the athletes, with Poland leaving a strong mark.

4.

Eleventh grade in 1976 and 1977 was also busy. I was under more stress since it was becoming apparent that we would be moving to Lublin to follow Father's professional advancement from the hospital to the university clinic. I was not happy; it meant significant disruption in my brother's and my private and academic lives, but it was a lesson in achieving maturity and evidently part of a bigger plan.

In July we went to a yachting camp in Dziewiszewo, a town known to us from the previous year a few kilometers west of Giżycko. I have good memories of the scouts' experience in Bytom, but otherwise felt sad that I would have to say goodbye to my friends, especially Teresa. I was also close to a classmate Ryszard (Rysiek) Bieda throughout high school, a friendship that survived forty years after I left Poland in 1983.

We left Bytom for Lublin on August 26, 1977, the Feast of Our Lady of Częstochowa.

Soon after, I started twelfth grade in Stanisław Staszic *Liceum* (High School), and my brother started the eighth grade in Jan Zamoyski Elementary School.

It was a challenging time for our entire family, and everybody had to make sacrifices to pull together, establish themselves in an unfamiliar environment, and move forward. Mother continued to work at the psychiatry university clinic for eight more years.

I finished Staszic High School on a high note. In addition to completing the required classes, there was a separate "maturity exam" (*matura*), which was a ticket to further studies and enrollment in college/university. The mandatory written exam was given in Polish literature and mathematics. There were two electives; I chose biology and English and did well on all of them with a 5 note.

June 1978 should have been a serious period of study for the entrance exam to medical school. I was distraught about the whole idea of finding oneself in Lublin and about temporary misunderstandings between our parents, and I spent the whole period of preparation with my mind wandering elsewhere. There was another FIFA World Cup in Argentina, and my habitual fandom started to interfere with a more serious attitude required in life. I managed to pass the exam satisfactorily enough, though, to be admitted among the first 200 candidates (out of approximately 800) to the School of Medicine in Lublin. Poland finished in fifth place in the World Cup, and Argentina won their first title.

Also in June, Polish cosmonaut Mirosław Hermaszewski went into space on the spacecraft Soyuz-30 and spent eight days aboard the Salyut-6 space station. Soviet (Byelorussian) pilot Pyotr Klimuk was the second cosmonaut on that mission.

In September we were required to work for the whole month at a construction site for the new apartment complex. Without completing this "practice," we would not have been allowed to start studying. It was a way to remind "the intellectuals" that this is still a "workers' and farmers' state" if not quite a "workers' and farmers' paradise." I always held physical labor in high esteem without special reminders needed.

Chapter 3

MEDICAL SCHOOL
IN LUBLIN

1.

The academic year started on Monday, October 2. We were led to expect an intense year of studying. The courses were initially in anatomy, biology, and medical propaedeutics, as well as other courses such as biophysics and statistics. Biochemistry and histology started in the second semester and continued in the second year. The head of the department of anatomy was Professor Mieczyslaw Stelmasiak, who was close to retirement at that time. The department had a high reputation for the level of instruction and study. (In June 1979, I finished the course with a note of 4+. My examiner was Dr. Irena Lize, and it was a good and fair result.)

Two weeks later, also on a Monday, the news of the election of a new Pope had reached Poland. I was returning home from Collegium Anatomicum in a bus line when a woman inside exclaimed loudly, "Cardinal Karol Wojtyła is the new Pope!" Somehow it did not strike me as very surprising. Something was in the air in the previous few days as we all knew the Conclave was happening in the Vatican. Wojtyła was fifty-eight at that time, and he was well known as a priest, philosopher, and poet engaged in the current political events as the right hand of the Polish Primate, Cardinal Stefan Wyszyński. As I arrived home that evening, Mother opened the door with a broad smile, and we hugged each other with great emotion.

People in Poland, including me, sensed this would effectively be the end of the post-war order, even if it were going to take some time to happen formally.

A week later, Cardinal Wyszyński visited the Catholic University of Lublin on its sixtieth anniversary, and I found myself just underneath the ambo of the chapel from which he gave the address to professors, the religious, and students. The sentence and the voice that still rings in my ears as if spoken yesterday declared, "We were supposed to come here together with Cardinal Wojtyła. Forgive me that I came by myself." This was greeted with a warm, hushed laughter.

The academic year went by quickly, and following June we took three days off to go to Warsaw to welcome John Paul II on his first pilgrimage to the native country. My three friends from medical school, Lechosław, Sławomir, and Grzegorz, and I took the train to Warsaw and pitched a tent in Łazienki Park, close to the facilities with running water. Another friend Wojciech couldn't join us.

On Saturday, June 2, 1979, John Paul II preached his famous homily at the Victory Square (currently Piłsudski Square) at the Tomb of the Unknown Soldier, reminding the Poles of their history and the faith that had carried them when the nation was "abandoned by the allied powers" during World War II. He said that without Christ it is impossible to understand the history of Poland and of the people who inhabited this land.

He ended with a cry as the Son of Poland and as a Pope: ". . . from the depth of the millennium, on the vigil of Pentecost, let your spirit descend and renew the face of the earth, the face of this land."

After these words, the applause lasted for at least fifteen minutes, with loud invocation from almost half a million throats: "We want God."

This was a demand to end the official atheist communism, which did not represent the soul of the nation. My later review of the newspaper commentaries showed clearly that *Pravda* ("The Truth") in Moscow, as well as *The New York Times* and *The Washington Post* tried to backpedal the significance of this event. Nothing was going to change in geopolitics according to these powerful men.

Wojtyła's warmth, charisma, and force of personality changed the history, but his later ecclesial policies and preferences were disappointing to me; he favored modern philosophies of personalism and phenomenology, approved of modern liturgy while not correcting abuses, and advocated for unbridled ecumenism and religious syncretism over traditional Catholic, Thomistic approach. By the end of his pontificate, the crisis in the Church became more visible, including sexual abuse problems. He appointed many very doctrinally questionable, weak bishops. My views of his Catholic guardianship evolved over the years from emotionally positive to disavowing in general. The Church is more than a personality cult of one pope, because it always must reflect Her Divine Founder.

In July, my brother and I traveled to Great Britain by train to visit our family in Edinburgh first and to see some of the riches of history and culture. It was our first trip to Western Europe. The lush green grass of The Meadows in Edinburgh is still etched in our memory, as well as the castle with St. Margaret Chapel and the figures of Robert the Bruce and William Wallace flanking the main gate with the inscription: *Nemo me impune lacessit* ("No one can harm me unpunished"). We were fortunate to stay for a month with Aunt Grace, Barbara, Anna, and Charles, his wife, Ann, and daughter "Little Anna," (a popular name in our family) and had precious time to talk, reminisce, and experience beautiful places in and around Scotland's capital. One of them was Holyrood Palace, located at the bottom of Royal Mile, at the opposite end of Edinburgh Castle. It has served as the principle royal residence in Scotland since the sixteenth century and is a setting for state occasions and official entertainment. The town of Kirkcaldy, located at the Firth (estuary) of

Forth, which opens to the North Sea, was impressive.

I rented books from the library about the history of the Soviet Union in the twentieth century, for the first time by Western authors, revealing the unvarnished truth about the evils of Communism, the monstrous criminality of Lenin and Stalin, the Purges, and the horrors of World War II.

Przemek and I once joined a soccer pickup game at the Meadows. There were four young men passing the ball for practice, and we suggested that one of them join us and play for fun and a little competition. We did that for about half an hour. Some goals were scored, and it ended in a draw. In London, on our way back, we hit the traditional places of interest such as Buckingham Palace and 10 Downing Street. (The prime minister's office was still accessible all the way to the door entry; the entire street was cordoned off by tall black steel gates in 1989, which obviously were there by the time of my next visit in 1996.) Madame Tussaud's Wax Museum, London Tower, River Thames, Hyde Park, the Houses of Parliament, and Big Ben (the bell of the Great Clock of Westminster) lived up to their reputation. I was cash-strapped by the end of the trip and could hardly afford to buy a can of Coke. My brother did better to save money.

The return leg to Warsaw on the train felt faster and easier than the outbound trip.

The second academic year started in October 1979. I met a priest at the Catholic University of Lublin, Fr. Jan Piotrowski, with whom I developed a friendly relationship. He was admitted to the hospital soon after we met, and I paid him a visit. His illness fortunately resolved, but his health required medical attention from time to time.

During the first year I tried to make friends with a young lady named Beata, and we spent time studying together. I invested more emotionally in her than she in me, but everything ended quickly. The first few months of the second academic year I was not looking for female friends, but in December, Dorota came into my orbit. She was also a second-year student. I was unhappy about my recent experience with Beata and held back emotionally in my relationship with Dorota, which was not good. On the other hand, I enjoyed the classes more than in the first year. Final exams in June 1980 yielded the 5 notes from all courses including histology, biochemistry, physiology, and history of medicine. There was also an English language course and Marxist philosophy. It was labeled as such, although it involved other themes, at least in abbreviated form, starting with the writings of Plato, Aristotle, Socrates, and St. Thomas Aquinas, and then continuing with Rene Descartes, John Locke, Voltaire, David Hume, Emmanuel Kant, and Soren Kierkegaard. The latter philosophers, starting with Descartes, with their empiricism and naturalism, paved the way for Friedrich Nietzsche and Karl Marx, who represented the ever more visible conflict between the supernatural and materialistic vision of life. There was a major fault line between these two viewpoints.

It was remarkably interesting that as I pondered about all these philosophical concepts, the conflict was about to take place in its tangible, visible form of a political struggle launched in the Gdańsk Shipyards and several other places starting in early July 1980. Political crisis and demand for change was felt everywhere as the economy was stalling; there were empty shelves in stores and political demands presented. It was an effect of rapid growth fueled by Western credits in the first half of the 1970s, but after 1976 the centrally planned economy was unable to use the added resources effectively. GDP growth was negative in 1979 and in the first half of 1980. Other major ports such as Gdynia, Szczecin, and Elbląg followed suit. The strikes took place in Warsaw, Kraków, and Silesia and in every other major industrial center in the country. One of the first to strike were the railway workers in Lublin. I experienced it firsthand because the scheduled train simply never took off one day in July, and I had to scrap my travel plans. It jarred for a moment, but we knew there was a larger cause behind this transformation, which was happening peacefully.

The crisis ran its course through August and ended with the signing of the Gdańsk Agreement. Its main signatories were Lech Wałęsa for the Strike Committee and Mieczysław Jagielski, deputy prime minister for the Communist government. There were twenty-one points or demands. The first and most important one was the acceptance of free trade unions independent of the Communist Party and of enterprises, in accordance with convention No. 87 of the International Labor Organization and concerning the right to form free trade unions, which was ratified by the Communist government of Poland.

It was a major victory for the forces of freedom, but clearly, major obstacles still lay in the way to obtain a better, more normal life in Poland. The government was weakened but not fully neutralized and ready to completely yield power, as we found out sixteen months later, in December 1981.

In early July, Przemek and I joined Olek in going to the town of Wołczyn, located forty kilometers north of Opole, west of Kraków and Bytom. There was a wooden church that Olek was tasked with restoring, and our role was to use kneaded bread to prepare and clean the walls and the grout to fill the cracks. Olek later would use his artistic skills and imagination to repaint the polychromies of the church.

On the TV evening news there were dramatic addresses delivered by Prime Minister Edward Babiuch, who had replaced Piotr Jaroszewicz in February, and later by Edward Gierek himself, who looked quite anxious. Both politicians encouraged the discontinuation of "work stoppages" (euphemism for "strikes") and a return to daily duties. The economic system, however, was not fair and fruitful for much of the population. Hence, it underwent a major transformation a month later.

The 1980 Summer Olympics in Moscow took place between July 19 and August 3. It was a strange spectacle, marred by the Western boycott led by the United States. The thirty-ninth US president, Jimmy Carter, reacted strongly to the Soviet invasion of Afghanistan. It was another chapter in an ongoing competition between the two superpowers. Only eighty countries participated in the Olympics, the smallest number since 1956. Sixty-six countries boycotted. Some of the athletes from the boycotting countries participated under the Olympic flag. (Among them were English runners Steve Ovett and Sebastian Coe, who won the 800 meter and 1500 meter, respectively). Despite the absence of the US athletes, some disciplines still maintained a remarkably prominent level. USSR and East Germany together won 127 out of 203 available golds (eighty and forty-seven, respectively). USSR won 195 total medals, and East Germany won 126. Poland won thirty-two medals overall but only three golds, giving them tenth place in the medal count. Władysław Kozakiewicz won the pole vault with the world record of 5 meters, 78 centimeters, and displayed a *bras d'honneur* gesture to the hostile Soviet crowd. In addition to the Iberian slap and Italian salute, in Poland it is officially known as Kozakiewicz's gesture. The public in Poland naturally appreciated it as a sign of defiance in the middle of the strikes and ongoing political crisis, in the Soviet Union it was obviously seen as an insult.

Bronisław Malinowski won the 3000-meter steeplechase, recovering from an approximately 40-meter deficit to Tanzania's Filbert Bayi until the last 150 meters. Unfortunately, he died in a car accident a year later in Grudziądz, Poland. Jan Kowalczyk won the equestrian competition. Jacek Wszoła placed second in the high jump. I watched these events with my medical school friend Marek and his fiancée, Małgorzata, in the Polish mountain village of Polańczyk in the Bieszczady Mountains, near the large Solina Dam, which created Lake Solina. River San supplies the lake; it lies very close to the Ukrainian border. It presented an excellent area to walk, bike, jog, and swim, which we certainly took the opportunity to do.

2.

In December 1980 (around the time of the report of John Lennon's death), Gosia appeared in my life. Her given name was Małgorzata Kotlińska, and we had been aware of each other's existence since 1978. That one day in December we felt attracted to each other very strongly and sensed that this was going to be a serious, lifelong relationship. We were in front of the Collegium Maius, one of the main medical school buildings and felt an "aura" surrounding us. We smiled and greeted each other warmly and said that it was good to meet. She wore an airy dress of green-yellow color with floral accents. Adding to the drama, I told Dorota a few weeks later, while admiring autumn scenery in the park, that my life would be changing.

Christmas and New Years were approaching. It was a time of enormous charm in the Lublin region; the feeling was intensified by our falling in love. The winter weather was perfect. There were a few inches of snow covering the ground, the trees, and the rooftops; it was not too cold. My family went to Kraków for Christmas, as we were used to doing throughout our Bytom and Lublin years. The entire family gathered there. Gosia and I spent New Year's Eve in the beautiful historic town of Kazimierz Dolny on the Vistula (Wisła) river, in a restaurant named *Dom Architekta* (The Architect's House). Gosia's brother, Bogdan, and his wife, Jola, were with us. We welcomed New Year 1981 with a customary glass of champagne and drove home to Puławy, Gosia's hometown, early in the morning, where I introduced myself to Gosia's parents, Stanisława ("Nina") and Ludwik.

Two months later we met in Kazimierz again, this time as a group of students/friends to celebrate the halfway mark (*półmetek*) through medical school. The restaurant was on the other side of the square from The Architect's House but equally charming. There were friendships, relationships, commitments, and foundations of future marriages being formed, and we had a fun evening.

Kazimierz is the name of a historic Jewish quarter in Kraków, and since it is located about 350 kilometers southward, up the stream of the Vistula River, it carries the name *Górny* ("Upper"). The one down the course of the river near Puławy is *Dolny* ("Lower"). It is named after King Kazimierz Wielki (Casimir the Great), the only one endowed officially with this moniker among Polish monarchs, princes, dukes, and kings between 966 and 1795. (Other kings such as Bolesław Chrobry (the Brave), Władysław Jagiełło, and Jan III Sobieski also achieved great political and military victories).

Third year ended quickly in June, and on finals I received a 5 in microbiology but only a 4+ in pathophysiology, which I remember taking extremely hard instead of with more humility.

May was a month of momentous events. On the thirteenth (the anniversary of the first apparition of Mary to three shepherd children in Fatima, Portugal, in 1917) there was an assassination attempt on John Paul II. The security forces quickly apprehended Turkish shooter Mehmet Ali Agca and arrested him. A mysterious nun had grabbed his hand after he fired two shots. Initially an obvious suspicion fell on the Soviets and the KGB, although it is known that the right-wing organization of Grey Wolves, with which Agca was associated, had training connections with the CIA. This whole event remains a mystery until today, and it may have been prophesied in Chapter 13 of the Book of Apocalypse: "If any man has an ear . . ."

On May 28, Cardinal Stefan Wyszyński died, and his funeral became a patriotic and religious demonstration. At least 500,000 people filled the streets of Warsaw, gathering again at Victory Square for the funeral Mass. Cardinal Agostino Casaroli, Vatican secretary of state, read the homily-eulogy in fluent Polish. I watched the entire event on TV.

We decided to travel with Gosia to West Germany and Italy in July and August to make some money and afterwards see Florence, Rome, and Venice. We took the train to Hannover and then hitchhiked further west to Cologne where we would work cleaning schools during the breaks for six weeks. Around Osnabruck we were able to hitch a ride with a very pleasant gentleman. Incredibly, we made a deeper connection and were later invited to visit him and his wife at their home around Bonn.

Their names were Hermann and Hannelore Hain. They gave us 100 DM, showed great hospitality, told us about Germany, and gave good travel advice. We corresponded with them for another two years after our return to Poland, until my departure for the US in September 1983. Sadly, we learned from Hannelore in one of her letters that Hermann died in an automobile accident in 1983. I wondered for a moment if Poland's sufferings from Nazi Germany forty years earlier were redeemed symbolically by the Hains' kind actions.

During our free time in Cologne, we visited the famous cathedral and attended Mass. It houses the reliquary of the Three Kings—distinguished foreigners in the Gospel of Matthew and Christian tradition—who visited Jesus after his birth, bearing gifts of gold, frankincense, and myrrh. Italy was beautiful. We visited St. Peter's Basilica and the Sistine Chapel. The tourists, including us, were so excited that the din inside the chapel became too loud after a while, and the security guards hushed everybody up. Indeed, the visitors should always maintain the proper decorum in the places of worship.

We managed to visit Florence, Assisi, and Francavilla a Mare, near Perugia. Sadly, we did not reach San Giovanni Rotondo, with the Sanctuary of Saint Pio of Pietrelcina (it is still on my travel bucket list). Throughout our trip, I shared with Gosia that I wanted to stay in the West, go back to Germany, or get to England and from there go to North America as a refugee. I asked Gosia to stay with me, but she was not ready. We then decided to return to Poland, talk to our parents about our serious plans, and do it the following year.

We hitchhiked our way from Cologne to Rome and back, and then to Venice and further on to Vienna. From there we took the train to Kraków. In Italy people were nice and exuberant. One gentleman said that "he was afraid to pick up strangers," and we learned Italian words such as *ho paura* ("I am afraid"). By the end of our ride together the ice was broken, the atmosphere warmed up, and he drove off honking and waving at us.

Vienna impressed us. St. Stephen's Cathedral is the symbol of the capital city, as well as the Imperial Palace Hofburg. The Cathedral Crypt has its bones and skeletons (a gruesome sight), and history. We tried to soak in as much as possible but also relax. There was a sports store in which I bought a pair of Austrian Kneissl skis at a deep discount. (The Austrian champion skier Franz Klammer used Kneissl skis during his career, including the Olympic downhill gold medal run in Innsbruck 1976). Gosia bought nice clothes. I used the skis in Szczyrk in the next two winter seasons and gave them to Olek in 1983.

Father flew to Columbia, Missouri, in early July for his second sabbatical and further work in nephrology, which was supposed to last for eight months, until February 1982.

3.

On Sunday, December 13, 1981, we woke to dramatically altered circumstances. The government drastically restricted everyday life by introducing martial law and a military junta to neutralize political opposition—the "solidarity" movement. General Wojciech Jaruzelski, who had been prime minister since February and the first secretary of the party since October, further consolidated his power, which became truly authoritarian. He announced the formation of the Military Council of National Salvation (*Wojskowa Rada Ocalenia Narodowego* (WRON)). The streets emptied out (except for the tanks). A dreary speech of the general's dashed the hopes of Poland's citizens.

The lettering of the Polish acronym WRON (*wrona* means "crow" in Polish) lent itself to jokes and epigrams such as *wrona orła nie pokona* ("the crow will not defeat the eagle"), a nod to the white eagle as the national symbol of Poland.

There was a break in studying for the rest of the calendar year. We managed to take the train to Kraków to spend Christmas at our family home. We had to show our internal ID cards at the checkpoints. Stores did not carry enough foodstuffs or other goods. Nevertheless, we felt the spirit of Christmas, which was giving us earnest hope.

In February 1982, a group of medical students decided to walk down the main avenue of the city of Lublin, Krakowskie Przedmieście (French: Cracow's Faubourg), as part of a city-wide demonstration against martial law. The ZOMO officer (an acronym for *Zmotoryzowane Oddziały Milicji Obywatelskiej*—Motorized Reserves of the Citizens' Militia) flagged me down and asked for my *dowód osobisty* (ID card). My name reached the dean's desk, and I had to come for a talk. The dean commented on my attempts to make myself a "hero" and said that when my father came back from Columbia, he wanted to have another conversation. I did not share our plans of wanting to leave Lublin and reunite in Columbia.

By then we had exchanged cryptic correspondence encouraging Father to stay in Columbia, from where he was supposed to return. We told him we would be working to join him there.

The spring semester of the fourth year went well. I received 5 marks from the most important courses in anatomic pathology and pharmacology, and 4s and 4+s in others. I remember my anatomic pathology teacher, Dr. Andrzej Stępień, very well; he made his subject interesting. Memorizing the material felt meaningful and important for future study and work.

The summer of 1982 was quickly upon us. The twelfth FIFA World Cup Espana 1982 started on June 13. It concluded on July 11 with the final between Italy and West Germany. Poland finished in third place again, tying with Italy, Cameroon, and the Soviet Union and beating Peru, Belgium, and France in the third-place playoff after losing to Italy 0:2 in the semifinal. It was almost counterintuitive for the team to perform so well in this political situation, but it paradoxically created an additional motivating factor. The core of the team was still strong with Grzegorz Lato and Andrzej Szarmach playing and scoring in their third—and final—successive World Cup; Zbigniew Boniek in midfield with Włodzimierz Smolarek, Stefan Majewski, and Janusz Kupcewicz backing him up; Władysław Żmuda (also in his third successive World Cup—he would make one more appearance four years later); Paweł Janas in defense; and Józef Młynarczyk in goal. The contributions of Jan Jałocha, Marek Dziuba, Andrzej Buncol, Waldemar Matysik, and Włodzimierz Ciołek were on par with other teammates, as there was a fourteen-player rotation in the basic squad. These players had enough talent and determination to be close to the top in the football hierarchy at that time. Antoni Piechniczek was a head coach; he was a worthy successor to Coach Górski.

In late July I decided to visit Chałupy again and prepared to drive from Lublin. Our car was a Fiat 126p, which we called the *maluch* ("baby" or "toddler"). There was no gasoline sold except on specially regulated coupons, twenty liters (five gallons) per month. An underground economy started to blossom very quickly, and one could buy a little more gas by "tipping" the gas station attendant.

The *maluch* got excellent mileage, about thirty-two to thirty-four miles per gallon, but it had two cylinders, twenty-three horsepower, and a maximum speed of sixty miles per hour.

I drove the whole distance of 600 kilometers (400 miles) in one uninterrupted stretch of eight hours (except for a quick refueling from the spare canister of twenty liters of gas somewhere in Masuria). Otherwise, I did not stop even for food or a restroom. The roads were empty. I encountered no more than fifty or sixty cars traveling in this whole part of the country that day.

In August we went for ten days to Lake Balaton. Father was in the United States, and Joanna joined us. This was a group of about thirty people; we had a high-end motor coach for the journey. One of the main purposes of the trip, if not the main purpose, was to call Father in Columbia, Missouri, and confirm more officially our desire to join him. I was the most forceful spokesperson of these intentions at that time. We were afraid that in Poland we would not be able to communicate freely because of possible wiretapping. In retrospect, it serves only as confirmation of how psychological operations of various totalitarian governments work.

There was an amusing episode when a couple of Polish-speaking vendors started selling inexpensive watches and jewelry toward the end of our trip. It was done in a clandestine way; they pretended at first to be regular tourists, but as the conversation focused on the opportune subject, they quickly produced their goods from underneath their towels. All the members of the trip bought something, but as we were getting close to the Polish border (via Slovakia), everybody grew concerned that customs would confiscate the items. We started putting them on our wrists and necks, as if we had previously possessed them. I kept my "trophy" watch in the box. Unfortunately, a few weeks later it was off by quite a few seconds during each twenty-four hour period.

In September Gosia and I went to Chałupy for two more weeks. The weather was noticeably different in July, with the temperatures around 55°F on average rather than 72–74°F. I ran long distances, setting out five kilometers eastwards to Kuźnica and back. Przemek came for a few days with his friend Wojtek, and they also used the forest path to exercise and run.

The fifth year of medical school was uneventful. I managed a 5 in the final exams in internal medicine and infectious diseases, but my thoughts were already in America. I did not share these intentions with many friends. Gosia certainly knew. We planned that, if possible, she would come to Columbia after graduating from medical school in December 1984. We believed that we could make it as a family and work in the medical field. In June 1983 I exchanged engagement rings with Gosia in Kraków. We felt joy but also had a sense of the obstacles in the way, some inside our family and others outside of it. We believed there was much to unite us, and that the supernatural bond (grace) would grow.

Cousin Charles visited Poland in May, spending time mostly in Kraków, but he also managed to visit us in Lublin. Charlie was a noted actor and stage director in Edinburgh and always very emotional and proud of his Polish heritage.

I was physically very inactive between September 1982 and June 1983. It was a reaction to the events outside, a feeling of disgust and discouragement. I was studying, sitting on a couch, and watching TV. I did not believe the programming was good, apart from the World Cup in June 1982. When I finally decided to break my self-imposed hibernation, my first brisk walk and run outside resulted in a jelly-like sensation in all my muscles. I made a quick decision to return to normal life, and in two to three weeks things were back to normal.

In August I joined Gosia and her parents for a vacation in Białogóra , about thirty-five to forty kilometers west of Chałupy. We used tents for the accommodations. There were facilities with running water available. The atmosphere of the Baltic seaside was always relaxing with clean, healthy air; cool, refreshing seawater; forest; and dunes. I had to delay my trip to Białogóra by about two weeks. Cousin Barbara from Scotland visited us again, but this time it somehow fell mostly on me to entertain her. She was incredulous of my plans to emigrate to America, and she wanted to preserve childhood memories one last time. We spent time in Kraków and visited Ojców National Park, with its historic Pieskowa Skała Castle. There is a tall limestone stack close to the castle called *Maczuga Herkulesa* (the "Bludgeon of Hercules") due to its distinctive shape. Throughout this time, I missed Gosia and was counting days and hours until I could reunite with her and her family in Białogóra , where they had been vacationing since the beginning of the month.

I had managed to obtain a Polish passport to travel abroad due to our mother's connections at the local department of the ministry of the interior. There was an additional fee ("gratuity") paid to the officer who later obtained permission from his superiors to issue the passport.

Chapter 4

AMERICA AND
MEDICAL EDUCATION

1.

On Monday, September 5, Gosia and I, along with my mother, drove to Warsaw. We had dinner and stayed at a hotel overnight; my flight would depart the next morning. Martial law ended in Poland on July 22, a Communist national holiday. The military junta had previously "suspended" it on December 31, 1982, but Poland was still under various sanctions from the US government, and there were no direct flights on LOT Polish Airline between Warsaw and New York or Chicago. The first leg of the trip ended in Bucharest, the capital of Romania. The flight to New York was on Romanian Airline TAROM. It used Soviet aircraft IL-62, which had had a fatal accident in Poland in 1980 and another one later in 1987. In New York I transferred to the domestic terminal at JFK airport and flew to St. Louis on TWA. Father was waiting at the gate. We greeted each other with joy and relief, although other family members' coming was still not a certainty.

A week before my flight, the Soviets shot down Korean Air Lines flight 007 from New York to Seoul over the Island of Sakhalin, a prohibited Soviet space that the plane had encroached by postulated navigational mistake. Georgia representative Larry McDonald was on board. He was known for his anticommunist views.

Father and I drove to Columbia, and I was grateful to be at my destination late at night, tired and thirsty.

The rest of September we tried to relax a little. I got to know the university town. It was picturesque, with hills, cliffs, and parks surrounding the bypass roads leading to the city center. I met my father's coworkers at the division of nephrology and wrote long letters to Gosia. I applied for a few not-for-credit courses which would prepare me linguistically and medically to formally enter the school of medicine. I was given credit for two years at the US medical school; hence the junior and senior years were awaiting. I was hoping to graduate in May 1985, but that proved to be too difficult, so the goalpost was later moved to May 1986. Nevertheless, I did many of the initial not-for-credit rotations with the students from the class of 1985.

We went to Lake of the Ozarks and enjoyed time in a rented boat, plus did a little swimming and hiking. Later we went to Kansas City and Independence to visit the Harry S. Truman Presidential Library and Museum. The climate was extremely hot and humid compared to the more moderate weather in Poland, but Columbia has four seasons, and positive aspects of warm, sunny weather—more serotonin and vitamin D production in the body, as well as less of the stress hormone, cortisol.

2.

I started my preparatory courses on Monday, October 3, 1983, from the tutorial in endocrinology. The material was not entirely new, but I had to relearn the terms and various descriptions and build an updated body of knowledge.

The news broke at that time that Lech Wałęsa was awarded a Nobel Peace Prize for his work as a trade union leader and a peaceful challenger of communism. The physicians and students I managed to become acquainted with were kind to offer congratulations.

I wrote a letter to the school of medicine in Lublin, notifying the dean of my desire to stay in the United States "for an extended period of time" and apologizing for not returning for the beginning of the sixth year of study. In their reply, the school of medicine in Lublin wrote that they would not welcome me back.

Subsequent courses were in infectious diseases, neurology, gastroenterology and cardiology. Cardiologists Dr. Brent M. Parker, Dr. Gregory Flaker, and Dr. Richard Webel awakened my early interest in this specialty.

In March 1984, my tourist visa expired; it had only been issued for six months. I received a visit from an FBI officer who asked me about my plans. I said that I would like to stay in America, study medicine, and live, work, and contribute here. There was certainly a moment of anxiety and tension: What would happen if the immigration service deported me? I could not imagine myself returning to Poland's drab reality. America was too attractive due to its sheer size. The theater of possibilities appeared so much greater—limitless. Everything here was on a much larger scale. Father's example was firmly in front of my eyes. If he could make a leap from being a modest, simple shepherd of cows in a small Polish village in 1940s to being a university physician in the United States forty years later, this should not be insurmountable for the next generation, who had already made progress on the shoulders of their ancestors. My green card (permanent residency card) came in the mail two or three weeks later. I was more than relieved and grateful for such an outcome.

I had reconciled myself to the possibility of a different outcome, namely that I would have to leave the US and wait for the green card in Poland. It would have delayed and derailed my plans. My medical career would have certainly been over. Life is a curious combination of coincidences, chances, and subjective decisions made by people in the circumstances they are facing. We must always respect laws, but laws should sustain, not hinder human progress when there is no evidence of malice (important clause).

In June I felt ready to sit for the MSKP (Medical Sciences Knowledge Profile) examination, which would enable me to enter medical school formally. I drove my father's 1983 Oldsmobile Delta 88 Royale Brougham to Chicago where the exam would take place. The exam used paper booklets, and the examinees were supposed to use a #2 pencil to mark the ovals with the correct response. I managed to pass quite well, and after receiving the scores and completing the last preparatory courses, I could finally start formal curriculum on November 19, 1984.

In the summer, Lake of the Ozarks again beckoned, with all the benefits nature had to offer. In July of that summer, Grandfather Lolek asked me to buy him a six-volume set of adventure books by German author Karl May. The books were about a fictional character, Apache Chief Winnetou, who gives his name to the trilogy, and his friend Old Shatterhand, a first-person narrator. Grandfather was a big fan. I also read his books in Polish in my very young years. I was pleased to do it for Grandfather; he passed away a year later. I wore a black mourning ribbon on the lapel of my white lab coat after his passing for almost three months.

In the fall I took advantage of the excellent running paths at MKT Katy Trail off Stadium Boulevard. Sometimes we got together with one or two friends and logged in the miles, trying to outrun each other at the end. I ran a 6:45-minute mile on one or two occasions. At twenty-five-years-old, one possesses peak physical powers, can control one's weight easily, and can recuperate quickly. My left knee was not showing any signs of trouble. We also had a soccer league in which the medical school faculty, students, and other players participated, but I sometimes took the competition too seriously and lacked social graces. Such was also my approach sometimes while playing cards or table games, for which I never had any aptitude. I am still embarrassed at myself for those few petty outbursts of frustration and immaturity.

I decided to start the final sixteen-month stretch from a second cardiology elective, this time devoted exclusively to the research project on hyperlipidemia and the risk of coronary artery disease. It was in large measure due to Gosia's planned arrival in Columbia at the end of December, and I wanted to have a bit more flexibility with my schedule. The elective took place in December and January, and in early February, I presented the findings of the project on a special university Student Research Day. The mentor of this project was Dr. Parker.

I was pleased to receive an award/stipend of $1,000, which would certainly help with the travel plans and daily expenses.

Simultaneously, Gosia and I were planning the wedding. I belonged by then to the Sacred Heart Parish after trying out other churches. We had the date of February 2, 1985, firmly planned, engraved on our wedding rings, and written on the invitation cards. The pastor, Fr. John Long, was immensely helpful and accommodating. We had a brief civil ceremony at the recorder of deeds office on Saturday, February 2. Unfortunately, the last church-related documents from Poland were delayed, and we had to wait with the church ceremony. The official church wedding was indispensable, in addition to the civil ceremony. Since we had already planned the rest of the month of February off and expected to have both civil and religious wedding ceremonies under our belts in order to enjoy a honeymoon, we decided to travel to the East Coast. We drove in an '82 Plymouth Champ through Louisville, Frankfort, and Lexington, Kentucky; to Richmond, Virginia; Washington, DC; and New York City. We enjoyed great monuments, buildings, museums, and parks of the capital city including National Mall, Lincoln Memorial, Washington Monument, and Arlington Cemetery. I had a picture taken next to the cardboard cutout of the 40th US president, Ronald Reagan. We walked by the Potomac River and drove to places of interest in neighboring Virginia and Maryland. We bought a beautifully edited Bible at the Polish bookstore in Bethesda. It is still in my possession thirty-eight years later.

New York City dazed us with its size, colors, dynamism, and special charm. We saw the musical *Cats* on Broadway and visited the King Władysław Jagiełło monument in Central Park. The Metropolitan Museum of Art provided a breathtaking experience with its permanent collection of works of art from classical antiquity and ancient Egypt.

We returned to Columbia at the end of February. I immediately had to start the required clinical rotation in internal medicine. Somehow, I felt mentally exhausted and uncoordinated at times. I felt that I was repeating this rotation, having done it in Lublin before, and I lacked full enthusiasm this time. I received a B grade on the final multiple-choice exam and overall.

On Saturday, May 25, we finally solemnized our union during a Catholic wedding ceremony at the Sacred Heart Church. We had already known that our first child was on the way since mid-March. The sad part was that Gosia was not getting acclimated in Columbia, and she decided to return to Poland to have our child there. This left me heartbroken, but I felt that there was nothing I could do. I had to maintain an attitude of equanimity, hoping that better times would return. I drove with Gosia to Chicago on June 15, and she boarded the plane to Warsaw at the O'Hare Airport. We promised each other to persevere, that we would see each other again once I was more established and earning money as a resident physician.

After returning to Columbia, I decided to rent a room with my friends, Janice and Timothy, becoming a lodger for about six months. (We still remain good friends today through Christmas postcards and Facebook messages. I visited them in Tennessee in 2001, shortly after the 9/11 attacks.) For the last six months of medical school, I had a room in the dorm.

In the final year of medical school, during July and August, I devoted myself wholeheartedly to the required rotation of general surgery. Compared to internal medicine in March and April, my attitude was enthusiastic since this was the rotation that I had not completed in Lublin. The instructor was Dr. Walter Kirt Nichols, and he demonstrated a versatile and decisive approach to surgical interventions. Likewise, the influence of Dr. Donald Silver, chief of the surgery department, had an impact on me in the technical and professional areas, as well as the human sphere. It was at that time that an "interventional" vocation took shape in my mind. If not surgery, then possibly interventional cardiology could be considered. This thought matured during the next three to four years.

I received an A on the final and on this rotation overall. It was a confidence booster. After surgery there was pediatrics, also with an A, and in the spring of 1986, I completed obstetrics-gynecology with a B.

In the meantime, I secured a spot in the internal medicine residency program at the University of Connecticut in Farmington. In November 1985, besides Farmington, I interviewed in two or three other hospitals in Washington, DC, and in New York. Farmington was an excellent destination.

On December 14, our daughter Ania (Anna Małgorzata) came into the world. I received a telegram from Gosia's father: "You have a daughter; they are doing very well." It was a bittersweet feeling. We were so far apart, and it took weeks to start receiving pictures. Phone connections were difficult.

In January and February 1986, I had a chance to follow Dr. Richard Schmaltz during cardiothoracic surgery rotation. It was an extremely gratifying experience to assist with the open-heart surgery, even if just holding the retractor. It broadened my horizons and made me aware of how important it is for good collaboration to exist between the interventional cardiologist and a cardiac surgeon. Dr. Schmaltz's dedication to his work impressed me.

Afterwards I drove to Winter Park, Colorado for three or four days of skiing. It was the first time I had skied in America, and my first practice in four years. I had a wonderful experience. I loved the mountains and snow, and I "caught the bug" anew to ski recreationally.

The second trip to Winter Park happened in December 1987. Already from Connecticut, I flew to Columbia for Christmas, then drove to our destination with Przemek in a white Honda. Unfortunately, while it was my turn to drive, I skid on a slippery road, turned over once, and ended up in the median on the right side of the car. I was unhappy, but fortunately the damage to the car was manageable. We had to patch up the rear window and use the spare tire, but we finished the trip with two or three days of wonderful skiing again.

The third trip happened in April 1988, just four months later. This time Grandmother Gena and her son-in-law, Olek, came to Columbia. I flew all the way from Hartford to Denver. The experience at Hartford Airport was comical because I was literally ten seconds late at the gate, just as the plane was pushing off and was still a foot away from the dock. I came running down the jet bridge, motioning to hold the plane, and the gate agent was merciful to do it. This situation would not happen nowadays.

There were two remaining required rotations left: obstetrics-gynecology, as mentioned before, and then psychiatry as the very last, which was a difficult study for me. The last electives I took in ENT (otolaryngology) and neurology (this time receiving credit), and the class was ready to receive diplomas on May 17, 1986. I had not gotten to know many of my classmates well because of being with them for only two and a half years and doing some electives with the class ahead of us. However, I expected to maintain contact with my classmates in the future.

3.

I drove to Connecticut and rented an apartment in Hartford, the capital city of the state. I liked the moderate climate, the closeness to the ocean, and a little more familiar-looking urban architecture.

Before the first year of the residency started, 13th FIFA World Cup, again in Mexico, attracted millions of fans and hundreds of commentators throughout the month of June. I connected with an acquaintance from the class of 1985 in Columbia, and we watched games at the sumptuous home of his friend, an attorney. Poland finished fourteenth out of twenty-four teams; Argentina won its second title.

At the end of the month, Gosia managed to visit me in Connecticut for two weeks. It was an emotional time; Ania was six months old and stayed with her grandparents. We met Polish friends Jolanta and Wesley, who pledged to help Gosia return to the US on a more permanent basis as soon as possible. Gosia already had her MD degree and worked as an anesthesia resident in Puławy. We persevered to build our relationship despite the difficulties and disappointments and the temptations that threatened it.

The internship year was intense and difficult. Gosia returned to Poland in mid-July, and we drove together to JFK airport. I was busy at the time with hospital service under the direction of an enthusiastic and exacting academic teacher, Dr. Andre Kaplan, a nephrologist. He and my father were aware of each other professionally, but it obviously had no bearing on my daily duties. I started to compare various medical approaches and worked to develop my own way. I intended to incorporate scientific divagations, using the formulas, probabilities, and algorithms in a humanistic approach, with a possibility of surgical or interventional solution and restoration of good health. Dealing with chronic medical conditions demanded patience, which my father excelled in; I had a "do the procedure and move on" attitude.

Dr. Kaplan gave me a positive evaluation from the rotation but also noted that my "priorities were sometimes misguided," undoubtedly referring to my driving Gosia to the airport that day, which required taking off early from work.

Later I had a chance to meet noted physicians and researchers, especially Dr. Arnold Katz, a professor of medicine, cardiologist, and physiologist, and an authority on the role of calcium in the contraction and relaxation of heart muscle.

In February 1987 I used two weeks of vacation to fly to Italy to fulfill my desire to see Pope John Paul II. I had seen him in person previously, in the mid-1970s at Wawel Cathedral, when he was still a cardinal in red cassock and surplice.

The trip to obtain the Italian visa in the consulate in New York was an adventure. The weather in New York was snowy and cold in January. I left the car in an unmetered parking lot and saw it towed away. I had to walk two to three miles to the big garage and pay the fee of $180 to retrieve it.

The group audience with John Paul II happened because Fr. Jan Piotrowski was in Rome at that time to complete his doctorate studies. He was kind to welcome me at the Leonardo da Vinci (Fiumicino) Airport and set me up at the quarters within the Catholic Church of the Byzantine Rite, *Santi Sergio e Bacco* ("Saints Sergius and Bacchus"). These saints had been early fourth-century Roman military officers and Christian martyrs in Syria. The church was located at Piazza Madonna dei Monti and was a good starting point for all excursions within the heart of the Eternal City. The first night I found a book about World War II and the Katyn Massacre, which was not a mentally soothing subject to read about.

There were two groups at the audience with the pope, one from France and one from Poland. I managed to enter the library with the help of Fr. Piotrowski, who convinced the administrator of the papal visits and curator of Polish pilgrims in Rome, Fr. Konrad Hejmo, to let me in.

The audience was a warm, well-organized event. Each participant received a Rosary and had an individual picture taken with John Paul II with a group picture at the end. I have excellent memories, but subsequently my enthusiasm for him waned.

I visited Perugia and Assisi with Fr. Piotrowski, including Basilica of St. Francis and Portiuncula, a small church within the Basilica of St. Mary of the Angels from where the Franciscan Order started. *Portiuncula* literally means "a small portion."

When I returned to Connecticut, I showed the pictures to my

friends and sent copies to the family in Poland.

4.

With the internship ending in June 1987, I could think about a fellowship and of Gosia's coming within the next twelve months. I saw advantages of staying in Connecticut, but always remembered the dynamic, decisive approach of the cardiologists and cardiac surgeons in Columbia and felt that this could be my professional home.

I traded in the '82 Plymouth Champ for an '87 Mitsubishi Mirage. Both cars were of a similar blue color. The Mirage was more modern and had soft cloth upholstery. I thought it would be comfortable for the time being.

In late June, just before the beginning of the second year of residency, I passed the FLEX (Federation Licensing Examination), in place since 1973. It was a two-day exam. I got up early in the morning and drove to the examination site in Boston, Massachusetts, wanting to save a night's charges at a hotel. I passed two parts of the exam with a comfortable margin. FLEX was a licensing exam. It enabled a physician to practice medicine in the United States. I needed it for career advancement and in the short run to be able to moonlight.

I liked the hematology-oncology division at University Hospital at that time, and even expressed my interest in looking at further fellowship training with them. However, two to three months later I realized that the original idea of cardiology would be the fulfillment of my original dispositions and professional desires. I was not socially gracious again on one or two occasions while discussing these choices with my cardiology and oncology mentors and only hurt my chances to smoothly further my career in Connecticut. I learned I must find the right balance between certainty and ambition on one hand and humility and resignation on the other. One evaluation in Connecticut mentioned "the quality of certainty, which was irksome to some."

In the fall of 1987, I applied to cardiology programs in Massachusetts, New Jersey, and Pennsylvania, which would start in 1989. I was not accepted. Taking the next career step would have to wait.

As mentioned previously, skiing in Winter Park with Olek and Przemek in April 1988 was terrific, but the April sun burned my face badly. I had blisters and terrible swelling of the face, which took a week to heal. One can never overestimate the value of sunscreen lotion. I would wait for my next skiing trip until January 1993, when I would go to Crested Butte, Colorado, from Wichita, Kansas.

The second year of residency ended on June 30, 1988. In June, there was a joyful event of Gosia's and Ania's coming to Connecticut; we moved to a two-bedroom condominium in West Hartford. I was glad to "graduate" from a studio apartment in Hartford and welcome my family in a more comfortable situation. It was still a temporary visit, not official immigration. They received the tourist visa owing to the help from our Polish friends from New Britain. Gosia was planning to go back to Poland in May 1989, and we awaited the green card (permanent residency card), which we hoped would be ready in September 1989. We immediately purchased an '88 Geo Metro as a second car. It served Gosia and Ania at the beginning, since they had shorter distances to cover, mostly to the store and to the park, and I was driving between places of work. I owe Gosia a debt of gratitude for her devotion to me and the family. There was still a life of work, atonement, and sacrifice ahead of me and all of us.

In August 1988 I had the privilege to be a research resident at Dr. Katz's laboratory, learning certain scientific concepts from his adjunct faculty, and see the scientific rigor with which he conducted and directed the work of research as well as his everyday kindness and smile.

In September we drove to Doylestown, Pennsylvania, to visit the city and the National Shrine of Our Lady of Częstochowa, a Polish American Roman Catholic shrine that was founded in 1953. It has a reproduction of the Black Madonna of Częstochowa, Poland. The heart of Poland's third prime minister, Ignace Jan Paderewski, who was also a pianist and composer and died in 1941 in New York City, is preserved there. We attended Sunday Mass in Polish and had a hearty Polish breakfast afterwards. We spent some time in the church's bookstore. The architecture and the entire cultural, historic, and religious atmosphere were uplifting for my family and me. I returned there six or seven months later, this time by myself.

The decision to select the fellowship program starting in 1990 had to be made before October. I applied to the University of Missouri-Columbia and to the programs in Massachusetts, New Jersey, and Wisconsin. The interview in Columbia went well, and I was pleased to find out in March 1989 that I would start the fellowship in July 1990. Around that time (I was vaguely aware of it, but did not dwell on it emotionally yet), there was a difficult communication between the Vatican (John Paul II and Cardinal Joseph Ratzinger) and Archbishop Marcel Lefebvre, a founder of the traditionalist Society of St. Pius X. There were discussions about the directions of reforms after the Second Vatican Council. Archbishop wanted to consecrate two bishops of a traditionalist mindset, to be able to say Mass in Latin and continue with all the traditional teachings related to it. He finally consecrated four bishops without the express permission from the pope. This caused the rift. My medical career prevented me from getting emotionally involved or even knowing many details at that time. I tried to understand both sides but had an awakening to tradition, which would become deeper several years later. John Paul II and Cardinal Ratzinger showed "generosity" toward the adherents of the Traditional Latin Mass, but for the first time in my life I thought that they could have arbitrated this specific agreement much better.

My classmates and I were senior residents and marched quickly toward the conclusion of residency. There was good camaraderie, and we were able to stand up for each other. There was an additional meeting every two months or so during which, under the guidance of a designated faculty member (family practitioner), we discussed our problems and challenges, worked to reduce frictions, and laid out broader plans. Again, at the end of the program I later bemoaned my negative attitude and social awkwardness when I suggested that this program had not met my expectations. Stress and bad mood are poor advisors when speaking publicly.

Another mistake I made during the residency was to moonlight too much. This resulted from a misguided desire to focus too much on money, ostensibly for Gosia and Ania, but also to "look strong" in the eyes of my family. Besides, a new car model always tempted me.

Again, lack of proper deference to my mentors at times, assuming a positive response from them when I was not sure of one or had not properly asked for one, cost me relationships and the current or future moonlighting jobs. The best medicine for hubris was to hear, "You are not welcome here; leave now."

Despite these mistakes, I have a pleasant memory of my time in Connecticut, a time of fight, survival, and growth.

5.

I planned to work in the emergency rooms while awaiting the start of the fellowship. However, in May 1989 encouraging news came that I would have a chance to spend a year at Griffin Hospital in Derby, Connecticut, performing the functions of chief resident. I was grateful to Dr. Richard Garibaldi, the director of the residency program, and Dr. James Freston, head of the internal medicine department, who decided on this nomination.

We replaced '87 Mirage with the silver '89 Mitsubishi Galant, as our family was growing.

We already made plans to go to Poland for two weeks, which would be my first return in almost six years. Big political changes were happening, freedom was dawning, and Communism in Central-Eastern Europe was on its way out. It was a busy fourteen days. We visited families in Kraków, Puławy, and Lublin, where we attended Gosia's nephew Robert's baptism ceremony. Gosia and I were godparents. I visited the graves of Grandmother Marianna in Cikowice, next to Grandfather Józef's, and Grandfather Karol in Kraków. That was the first opportunity to pay a visit to their graves since their passing in March 1985 and July 1985, respectively.

We managed to go to Białogóra again to bring back the memories of 1982 and 1983. We used Gosia's father's Fiat 126p *maluch*, and I stressed the gear ratios in this poor little vehicle, being by now used to the powerful American cars. The car had to have the alternator replaced after returning home. Our accommodation was still in a tent. Freedom was in the air, but foodstuffs and services were still extremely spartan. There was a grill in the village, which used a very heavy, regenerated oil for fish and fries, and we suffered from gastrointestinal symptoms.

Gosia and Ania stayed for the summer. I flew back to Connecticut to finish the residency and then interview and prepare for chief residency in Derby.

6.

My daily commute from West Hartford to Derby was forty-five to fifty miles, and it required an effort to get up early and merge with traffic heading south in the morning and back north in the evening.

The traffic was usually heavy, and it resulted once in a side collision that damaged the recently purchased Mitsubishi Galant. I had to cut in front of someone because of road branching and paid for it by having the left side of the car rammed into a couple of times. While the retaliation was gratuitous, there was my part in causing it.

Haste while driving is not helpful. I must admit that in these early years in America I frequently showed impatience and a tendency to be reckless while driving. I continued to moonlight while working as chief resident and once had to forfeit my entire day's (or night's) pay for a speeding ticket. I tried to appeal it in court, with even worse effect. The nonsense of such an approach is fully evident in retrospect.

After four months, I made a connection with a resident physician who also lived in the Greater Hartford area, and we began carpooling, which saved gas and effort overall. He was from Thailand. We found common subjects to discuss while driving.

In September 1989 I became board-certified in internal medicine. I took the test at the University of Connecticut building in Farmington. It was another difficult multiple-choice test, and it would be the last year that the certification would be issued for a lifetime without the need to recertify every ten years. I was elected as a member of the American College of Physicians in December.

This was a rewarding year. I found out again that I tended to be peremptory and impatient with discussions and negotiations. I ate the humble pie afterwards, and toward the end of the year managed to relax quite a bit.

Living with my wife and daughter was a great reward and joy. But because of the stress, sedentary lifestyle, and constant driving, I had gained around thirty-five pounds. My brother finished medical school in Columbia at that time and married his fiancée, Katarzyna (Kasia) Wawszczak, also a medical doctor. The civil ceremony took place in Chicago, and the church wedding liturgy occurred at St. Nicholas' in Kraków. Unfortunately, Gosia and I could not join in celebrations in person, but good wishes always abound for one's next-of-kin. Przemek and Kasia continued their residency and fellowship training in Chicago.

In June 1990 it was time to pack our belongings and head to Columbia, Missouri. The market for our condominium was down, and I tried to rent it for a while, hoping to recoup its value at least partially. Finally, we had to sell it at a loss in 1991.

7.

We drove from West Hartford to Columbia in two cars. Gosia was pregnant with our second child, and the journey was difficult for her. Ania was riding with mom all the time. We stopped for an overnight rest in Columbus, Ohio.

Dr. Karl T. Weber had been recently appointed chief of the cardiology division in Columbia. He specialized in cardiopulmonary exercise testing and in the cardiac collagen matrix, exploring the role of cardiac collagen in heart failure. His closest collaborator was Dr. Joseph S. Janicki. The faculty members from my student years, Dr. Parker, Dr. Flaker, Dr. Webel, and Dr. Villareal remained at the core of the division, with Dr. Mustoufi as a new addition. This ensured strong clinical research and didactic framework for all activities.

My inner voice was telling me that despite the importance and attractiveness of research work, I wanted to be a practitioner, at least in the beginning, and look into invasive cardiology as a service to patients. Therefore, my time spent in the cardiac catheterization laboratory was important. I learned pacemaker terminology, functions, and settings; had a firsthand experience with the catheters and angioplasty balloons (stents were not available at University Hospital yet); and started becoming familiar with echocardiography.

Cardiology fellows read the electrocardiograms and exercise stress test procedures daily. Outpatient clinics are a source of education, while helping patients by working to solve their problems.

Our first son, Adam Karol, was born on August 14. What a tremendous joy to be finally present at the birth of one's child! Gosia, Adam, and I promptly returned home to our townhouse apartment on Imperial Court. Ania warmly welcomed her brother. Our home had a good-sized backyard, and the kitchen provided ample space for our needs, with a bar counter layout and a dining area in front. We could host up to eight to ten guests comfortably. We invited colleagues from the cardiology fellowship program for dinner on two or three occasions, and invited the family to celebrate our sons' births and baptisms.

Gosia's mother came soon thereafter to help take care of Adam. She stayed with us until late November. We drove to Chicago to see her off to Warsaw. We found time to go to the Polish Consulate on North Lake Shore Drive and cast absentee votes in the Polish presidential election. I voted for the former Solidarity leader Lech Wałęsa; my mother-in-law preferred the more liberal prime minister, Tadeusz Mazowiecki, in office since 1989. So, our votes "cancelled each other out." Mazowiecki finished only third, and there was a runoff election between Wałęsa and a Polish Canadian businessman named Stan Tymiński. Wałęsa won 75 percent of the vote and became the first democratically elected president of Poland since May 1926. He served one term of five years.

My mother-in-law returned to Poland, but we would soon see each other again in Puławy.

I received time off for Christmas. We flew to Poland on December 23 to show Adam to the rest of the family. He travelled in a small cot in the first row of the main cabin. We spent time in Puławy, Kraków, and in the Tatra Mountains, including Zakopane and Bukowina Tatrzańska. We managed to ski for a day or two with a cardiologist, Dr. Franciszek Monies, my father in-law's friend from Puławy.

I offered to share my experiences in thrombolysis and my progress in angiography and angioplasty with the faculty and students at the school of medicine in Lublin during grand rounds at the university hospital on Jaczewski Street. The audience received me with attention. Interesting questions and discussion ensued. Two former colleagues, who were excellent students in medical school and accomplished doctors, were kind to offer congratulations during the social part.

We welcomed the beginning of 1991 in Poland and returned to Columbia in mid-January. I returned to my duties in earnest, but I sensed that my connection and understanding with faculty members, especially the head of cardiology, had become strained and was eventually lost.

Taking time off was, in retrospect, detrimental for my settling in at the cardiology division in Columbia. I had this time off officially approved, but the doubt had been cast on my intentions to stay at University Hospital as a future faculty member. Indeed, the wheels had been set in motion to move on from Columbia after two years.

On March 25, Archbishop Marcel Lefebvre died in Martigny, Switzerland. It was a symbolic date and time (the beginning of the Holy Week leading to Easter). I did not follow these events directly at that time, but future developments would make me reflect on them in depth. I later increasingly appreciated the archbishop's courage in preserving the treasure of the Church, the Latin Mass.

In addition to the duties of the fellowship training, I moonlighted in the emergency room of the hospital in Harrisonville, Missouri. The drive was 120 miles from Columbia through Kansas City, with an additional 20-25 miles after that. I replaced the Metro with a black '91 Galant VR-4 that had a turbocharger and additional horsepower. One night I tried to get back home as soon as possible and did at least 105 to 110 mph close to Columbia. A trooper chased me down and looked at me with bemused incredulity. The ticket stood $150, but fortunately there were no further repercussions.

On October 4, I received American citizenship at a district court building in Kansas City, having passed the examination a few weeks earlier. The official swearing-in ceremony went very well, and I felt more secure and established in my new life in America as I poured out all my emotions and strength while reciting the Pledge of Allegiance. I applied for and received a US passport in the spring of 1992. (I have renewed it regularly every ten years; it is currently in the fourth iteration, valid until 2032.)

Our second son, Aleksander Marian (Alek), was born on January 3, 1992. We celebrated this time, as Gosia returned home from the hospital in two days. Her mother came again from Poland to help us with the baby and the growing children. She stayed almost until Easter, and we drove again to Chicago O'Hare Airport for her return to Warsaw. A week before Mom Nina's departure, I attended the American College of Cardiology in Dallas, Texas.

Both our sons were baptized by Fr. John Long at the Sacred Heart Church where we were married in May 1985. (My friend Rysiek Bieda was Alek's godfather; his godmother was Gosia's friend Anna Gajda from Puławy. They both fulfilled their function remotely.) Alek's first trip to Poland would take place in the summer of 1994. There were two more years of cardiology fellowship awaiting. It is hard to deny that the time commitment to the training in cardiology was heavy, and the family frequently came in second. The time off in December of the first year was an aberration; it had happened by accident, and it did not serve us well during our time in Columbia.

In April 1992 I learned that I should pursue the remainder of my fellowship in clinical track rather than stay for the third year in Columbia in laboratory research. An opportunity arose to go to Wichita, Kansas, and continue training with PTCA preceptorship in a leading cardiology group. This was a very satisfactory realization of professional plans. Desire to achieve financial stability for the family was one of the main motivators in choosing this career pathway. The observations of the realities of the medical world suggested that one would achieve it faster in clinical rather than academic medicine, at least initially. My internal clock wanted to pick up a faster tempo. In retrospect, there was a price to be paid for that. I learned that life is a lengthy process, that one must pace himself smartly, and that too much of a competitive attitude may come back to bite us later. I was the only breadwinner in the family; Gosia had agreed to be a stay-at-home-mother, and this situation colored my thinking, too.

Driving to Wichita took us through Kansas City where we had friends, a Polish couple, Wojciech and Teresa Varanka. They were a few years older than us and were Adam's godparents. They also worked in medicine. We enjoyed visiting them on every occasion and going to one of the lakes or parks in the city. I had by then bought a sports car, a red '92 Mitsubishi 3000GT VR4 (300 hp), for which the black Galant VR4 (250 hp) made room. The family car was still the silver Galant, and it soldiered on.

8.

It did not take long to get acclimated to Wichita. The medical group was very welcoming. There was a female cardiologist, Dr. Michelle Brown, who did the fellowship in Columbia a year before me. I owed her a good, smooth introduction to the systems in Wichita.

We lived on Rock Road, in a townhome apartment. We went to St. Magdalen's Church; it was a building that looked like a big cheeseburger, located at Woodlawn and Kellogg streets.

The work was rewarding. I observed and sometimes assisted in high-quality interventions. I saw patients in a busy clinic and always took the time to discuss risk factor modifications with them. The current technologies, such as noninvasive tomographic cardiac imaging, were still developing at that time, but cardiologists used ECG stress testing and echocardiography (resting and stress) daily. There was effective communication between the noninvasive and invasive or surgical specialties.

In October, Gosia and I had the opportunity to take a week off to go to Colorado, where we visited a resort in Vail. We did not stay there, though, choosing instead an economy hotel out of town. It was still before the opening of the ski season. We walked and hiked. Vail's altitude of 8,200 feet above sea level caused mild symptoms at first—a headache and shortness of breath.

In January 1993 I drove to Crested Butte, Colorado and stayed for three nights at a condo made available by Mr. Stan Stirling, the clinic administrator.

Around that time, Medcenter One Hospital in Bismarck, North Dakota, contacted me about a job opportunity for a recently trained cardiologist to join their team as a hospital employee; the recruiting effort came from the administration side of the medical system. Later I found out that physicians were not that enthusiastic about hiring new partners, feeling that it would cut into their earnings. I responded positively. The salary offered was attractive, as was the overall situation and geographical location. However, it turned out that my current year in Wichita would not count as an ABIM (American Board of Internal Medicine, Cardiovascular Specialty) accredited program, and I would have to go for a final year of such. A position at the Louisiana State University in New Orleans opened, and I regretted leaving Wichita so soon, but we planned the move.

In April 1993, toward the end of my preceptorship in Wichita, we prepared for a street 5K race organized by St. Francis Hospital. There were hundreds of people participating, of all age groups, including our entire cardiology group. I finished in the middle of the pack, with a time of twenty-three minutes and fifty seconds. I had been running recreationally in Wichita and did not feel any trouble with my left knee.

Also that month, we received the news that Father had received the Annual Torchbearer Award from the University of Missouri, acknowledging his contributions in research and didactics. We flew to San Diego, California, for the ceremony, which took place on Saturday evening at the Hyatt Hotel. Besides Mother, Przemek, Kasia, and myself, our family from Kentucky, Basia and Marshall, marked this occasion, which gathered a group of academics and nephrologists. It was a brief but gratifying time to pause and celebrate.

A farewell/welcome ceremony for several physicians occurred at the end of June at a hotel in Wichita, and I felt we'd received more from the group than we had given in return. A few months later, the sad news of Mr. Stan Stirling's untimely passing reached us in New Orleans.

We traded the red 3000GT VR4 for a green one in May; it represented modest savings in terms of monthly payment. But despite it being a new car ('93 model), there was a strong odor of cigarette smoke on the upholstery. I do not know why I went ahead with that deal, but the savings and the more agreeable color played a role, and I later managed to finally get rid of the undesirable odor inside the car. We also finally traded the silver Galant for another Mitsubishi, a front-wheel drive Diamante wagon, as the children were growing. It accommodated three or four big suitcases and other belongings.

9.

The fourth year of my cardiology fellowship in New Orleans was a necessary, solid combination of theory and practice to make me more confident in becoming an independent medical decision-maker for my patients in twelve months. I knew that the cardiology group in Bismarck was small, and I would not have a chance to hide behind my colleagues' backs, that the responsibility would be mine. Of course, I expected to seek their backup with tasks beyond the limits of my training and capabilities. Invasive cardiology leaves a small margin of error at times.

Dr. D. Lucas Glancy was the head of cardiology. A tall, imposing figure, he was very fatherly in his demeanor and inspired confidence and trust. There was enough time to train in diagnostic cardiac catheterization and observe Dr. Glancy perform angioplasty procedures, as well as benefit from the experience and dedicated effort of every faculty member. A first-year fellow, Dr. John Winterton, took the time to show me around the campus, the University Hospital (previously known as Hotel-Dieu), Touro Infirmary, and Charity Hospital of New Orleans. He was a good guide and steeped in the local culture. It helped me to get acclimated to New Orleans quickly.

We had seminars and grand rounds, and the trainees gave presentations on the topic of their interest to fulfill the requirements of the program. In the spring of 1994, I gave a presentation and spoke about the long-term results of coronary artery bypass grafting (CABG), reviewing the literature back to the early 1980s. Recent online articles demonstrate again that younger adults who underwent CABG had lower long-term mortality and incidence of adverse cardiovascular events than older patients. However, there is a price to pay in that the freedom from subsequent myocardial infarction or revascularization is lower in the younger patients. (Older patients are more likely to die in general of other, unrelated causes and will not count as a CABG failure.) Coronary artery disease, once developed, is a lifelong problem, and it is unlikely that if someone has a stent or CABG around the age of fifty, or even before, that they will not need repeat interventions at some point.

I had not stayed connected with my former residency and fellowship programs on a frequent basis, but I learned that Dr. Katz died in 2016. The news came from the University of Missouri of the passing of Dr. Silver and Dr. Parker in 2021. Dr. Glancy passed away in 2022. Writing this memoir and gathering memories is invaluable; it puts life in a proper perspective.

The subsequent history of New Orleans included exceedingly difficult experiences, which are still fresh in my memory. After Hurricane Katrina in 2005, the state government decided not to reopen Charity Hospital in its original location. Also, Hotel Dieu closed in 2015, and the new hospital was named University Medical Center of New Orleans.

Living in New Orleans for a year was an experience that cannot be compared to any other. We rented a house on Glenwood Avenue in Harahan, about twelve miles west from downtown New Orleans, next to the Colonial Golf Course and the Mississippi River Trail. I used the trail to run quite a bit on free weekends, and we walked there together as a family (Adam and Alek with the help of a stroller at times) as much as possible. Ania received her First Holy Communion in May 1994 at St. Rita of Cascia Catholic Church, a mile east of our home. Gosia and the children usually attended Mass there. I regularly went to other beautiful, historic churches: St. Anthony of Padua or Our Lady of the Rosary.

We visited Bourbon Street, downtown in the heart of the French Quarter, giving it a passing look. The walk took us to Jackson Square with its soaring St. Louis Cathedral and the equestrian statue of the seventh US president, Andrew Jackson, a treat for someone like me who is interested in history.

We were aware of a relatively high crime rate in New Orleans, and I found out that a female fellow in cardiology at Tulane University became a murder victim during that time, likely during an attempted robbery. I was on call that night and had to drive to the hospital to see a patient. The tragedy happened around that time and close to the pharmacy where I briefly stopped to buy something. The faculty informed us about this tragic incident the next morning.

The year in New Orleans quickly came to its conclusion. In June 1994 we were gripped by the news of the murders of Nicole Simpson and Ron Goldman. OJ Simpson was accused of murder and subsequently stood trial. We watched the low-speed police car chase of the suspect in Los Angeles on June 17. NBC interrupted the broadcast of Game 5 of the NBA Finals between the Houston Rockets and the New York Knicks to show the chase.

Soon after, we again packed up and got ready to drive to Bismarck, North Dakota, as I had worked out the details involved in the previous offer. A big moving van took the Mitsubishi 3000, our furniture, and all other belongings, while we all rode in the Diamante. The trip happened in two stages. First we drove from New Orleans to Chicago, about 950 miles, and from there Gosia and the children flew to Warsaw, Poland, to spend two months in Puławy. I drove by myself from Chicago to Bismarck, a distance of 840 miles.

Chapter 5

PRACTICE OF HOSPITAL CARDIOLOGY

1.

I found Bismarck very quaint, at ease, and different from any other place I had been to so far. The air was unmistakably "northern," with a cool breeze in the evening, a distinct contrast to the humid, warm air of the Mississippi Delta and the Gulf of Mexico.

The capitol and North Dakota Heritage Center, with the state museum, were close to State Street, the main north-south thoroughfare of the city. The streets were wide and clean, and they connected the city in a logical fashion. The Missouri River added character (and boating opportunities in the summer) and provided an opening to the "wild, wild west."

I found the house that we had arranged to rent while in New Orleans and waited for the moving van. It arrived in a few days, and I busied myself setting everything up and preparing to welcome the family. The house was small but warm and cozy, and we could raise a family in it.

Of course, the work started almost immediately, divided between the outpatient clinic, cardiac catheterizations, ECGs, stress tests, and echo labs. An outreach clinic in Watford City (180 miles northwest) completed my scope of responsibilities. My colleagues Dr. Ivaldo Lunardi and Dr. Walter Frank were helpful but demanding. There were good and tough moments in our interactions, and I had to earn the spurs every day. At the end of July, I flew to Columbia, Missouri, for the weekend with my parents and the visiting family from Kraków: Joanna, Basia, and her daughters, Justyna and Karolina. We went to the Lake of the Ozarks and had an enjoyable day walking, hiking, and renting a pontoon boat.

I took two weeks off after six weeks of work to go to Poland and return with Gosia and the children. I drove Diamante to Chicago and flew to Warsaw via LOT Polish Airlines. The first night we stayed at the newly built Marriott Hotel on *Aleje Jerozolimskie* (Jerusalem Avenue), one of the principal streets in Warsaw, in the east-west axis. We had a family gathering with Gosia's parents, Bogdan and Jola, another relative of my father-in-law, and of course the five of us. We had a refined dinner at Floor No. 2 restaurant, and I marveled at how quickly the economic situation of the country had been improving. Warsaw was still far from the modern metropolis it has become since 2000, and the Stalinist Palace of the Culture and Science was still the tallest building in the city. (There is only one taller as of 2023, Varso Tower, which is 1,020 feet tall. The palace stands at 778 feet.) We visited the historic center of the capital city, nearly destroyed in World War II and meticulously rebuilt with an enormous effort of the citizens from 1945 to 1950. The Old Town Marketplace, St. John's Archcathedral, Castle Square with King Sigismund's Column, and the Royal Castle are historic gems. (The Royal Castle was built in 1598 and demolished in 1655 to 1656 during the Swedish wars and in September 1944 by the German army. It was rebuilt only in 1971 to 1984, when it finally regained its seventeenth century appearance.)

We went to Białogóra again; my father-in-law generously offered us his Mazda 323 diesel. Ryszard, his wife Halina, and their two sons, Michal and Andrzej, joined us for the weekend. We enjoyed long walks by the dunes and recalled the good times in school and in scouts.

Bogdan also joined us later in the second week. We visited Kraków at the end of our stay. Grandmother Eugenia passed away the previous October, and we paid a visit at her grave, next to Grandfather Karol's.

The return to Bismarck was smooth. We usually flew through Amsterdam and Minneapolis via KLM-Northwest Airlines during our Bismarck years, but in the first two years, we sometimes chose to fly LOT to Chicago, including this time. We stopped for a day in the Windy City, spent the afternoon on Navy Pier, and visited North Lake Shore Drive and the Field Museum of Natural History. I also went to the Polish consulate to renew my passport. It was a symbolic way to show a connection with my heritage and to facilitate the border proceedings when returning to Poland in the future. It was always possible, however, to travel to Poland only on the US passport.

My new Polish passport was good for another ten years, until 2004. Then I would have a break until November 2009 before renewing the passport.

After taking care of all the administrative details, we returned to Bismarck in the Diamante. Ania started the third grade, Adam attended kindergarten, and Alek was still with Mom at home, getting ready for preschool. I was appointed clinical assistant professor of internal medicine at the University of North Dakota (Grand Forks) in September.

The first year of work went by fast. The winter was very harsh. We had to trade the green Mitsubishi 3000GT VR4 for a '95 Geo Tracker with a manual four-wheel-drive in the spring of 1995. Deep furrows of snow obviously made it impossible for the low-lying sports car to go through, but the Tracker sat high on its truck frame.

In early April we went to Big Sky, Montana, to ski over a long weekend. We used the Diamante and rented the equipment at the base of the mountain. We stayed at the Lodge at Big Sky, which had slope-side ski access and a short walk to shops and eateries at the Big Sky Resort. Gosia and I skied conservatively as we watched the children. Ania felt comfortable on her first skis. Adam did well on the children's slope, and Alek walked beside us bravely with his skis on. We had a good, albeit brief stay.

In May 1995 I passed the American Board of Internal Medicine cardiovascular exam, making me a board-certified cardiologist. The location of the examination was in Bloomington, Minnesota, inside what was then the Thunderbird Hotel near the Mall of America.

In June 1995 we welcomed Gosia's parents to Bismarck. I volunteered to drive them in the Diamante all the way from Chicago to Bismarck, for a chance to see the countryside better from the car. We stopped in Tomah, Wisconsin, for an overnight rest, which would become our hub on future trips.

We visited the state capitol and North Dakota Heritage Center and State Museum, as well as the Custer House in Fort Abraham Lincoln State Park in Mandan, a handsome, wooden two-story home with a wide front porch. It had all the areas and space needed for the proper home of a fort's commander. The Fort Abraham Lincoln Foundation, using Custer's own plans from 1874, rebuilt the house in 1989. Time had "stopped" there in 1875, and the guides recreated the appearance and atmosphere, reenacting the fateful day when General George Armstrong Custer headed toward Montana where he and his entire regiment would meet their fate at the Little Bighorn on June 25, 1876. The guides "reassured" the visitors that the general had "just walked out of the house" but would "return soon."

We visited the house and the museum on subsequent family visits, and the reruns were just as enjoyable as the first time, always revealing something else we hadn't known.

My in-laws and I then drove to the Badlands. We visited Medora but skipped the Medora Musical because of the timing and schedule. (I later would make this trip twice more, seeing the musical both times. The first was in June 1999 with my father-in-law, Ludwik; my brother-in-law, Bogdan; and Gosia and our children. We all fit in a three-row Lincoln Navigator that time. I went again in July 2003 with my cousin

Bożena, my father's niece.

I rented a car for the Badlands trip with the in-laws. Gosia and the children stayed in Bismarck. The school year had barely ended. Gosia needed the Diamante, and she was not comfortable in a Tracker. We drove Route 85 south to Spearfish, Deadwood, Lead, and Rapid City. We went to Mount Rushmore, in Keystone, South Dakota, and admired this great American historic landmark. The work of Gutzon Borglum and his family, friends, and collaborators—as well as that of the four hundred workers who labored for eight dollars a day on the mountain for fourteen years until the project's completion in 1941—defies credulity.

We returned to Bismarck for the last day or two of my in-laws' stay and then drove them in the Diamante to Chicago for their flight to Warsaw. As I look back at the time between 1982 and 2020, the number of trips I undertook by car is amazing. Assuming I drove fifteen thousand miles per year for thirty-eight years, it adds up to almost six hundred thousand miles. If the equator's circumference is 24,900 miles, it means that I have circled the earth almost twenty-three times in an automobile. One should add air travel and travel by boat to that number. (Only in the last three years have I slowed down on driving significantly, although there is an occasional trip from Sioux Falls to St. Paul, Minnesota, and to Kansas City, Missouri). In the last eight years I have finally been doing more walking and running, which I should have done all along.

My second year of work passed uneventfully. I was gaining experience with percutaneous interventions and established connections with the representatives of the leading pacemaker companies, Medtronic, St. Jude Medical, and Boston Scientific. In the fall I was elected fellow of the American College of Cardiology.

During my tenure in Bismarck, I became friendly with the pacemaker company representatives and occasionally went to dinner with them. We particularly liked Peacock Alley with St. Jude Pacesetter colleague Denny Newell; we had separate tabs. It was then, in my mid to late

30s, when I noticed that rich food with a glass of wine was causing a stiffening of my muscles and joints after dinner. These were, in retrospect, the first signs of elevated uric acid, to which I should have paid more attention. (The dinners with pacemaker companies ended in 2001 while I was in Minot.)

In the spring of 1996, we traded in the Tracker for a big GMC Suburban. The 5.7 L V-8 engine was making "only" about 230 hp (current engines are more efficient), but its roominess and safety were incomparable.

The summer of 1996 allowed us the opportunity to fly to Great Britain. It was the first visit for me since our initial voyage with Przemek in 1979, and the first as a family. We drove to Minneapolis-St. Paul in July, left the Suburban at the long-term parking lot, and flew to London Heathrow Airport and from there to Glasgow. We rented a car with the steering wheel on the right side, as the driving is on the left side in Great Britain. It was a five-door French Peugeot, and it served us well. I experienced a short learning curve to drive on the opposite side of the road from what is used in the United States and the rest of Europe.

We stayed at the Holiday Inn in the city and visited with our family daily over the next four days in Edinburgh, incorporating short excursions in and outside of the city, retracing the itinerary of the 1979 visit. The Castle, the Royal Mile, Holyrood Palace, Firth of Forth, The Meadows, and Kirkcaldy again made an impression. The air was quite chilly in July in Scotland, but I preferred short dress pants instead of long jeans, being in a minority. I felt comfortable in a long-sleeved shirt and a nylon jacket, which protected me from the elements. Everybody else was wrapped up.

One evening we gathered at a long-established and fashionable Scottish restaurant that served haggis, which is a savory pudding containing sheep's pluck (entrails), onion, oatmeal, suet, spices, and salt mixed with stock (broth) and traditionally encased in the animal's stomach. Barbara, her husband Patrick, Anna, Charlie and his daughter

Anna, Marion (a cousin from Aunt Grace's side) and her husband, Ian, were present. They all showed their heart and hospitality.

The time came quickly to depart for London. The best and the quickest road is the A-1, which is the longest numbered road in the United Kingdom, at 397 miles (639 kilometers). It passes through Berwick-upon-Tweed, Newcastle upon Tyne, Sunderland, York, Peterborough, Huntingdon, Hatfield, and North London, among other towns and cities. The trip was smooth, provided splendid views, and felt safe.

We checked in at another Holiday Inn on Kensington Street close to the city center. The River Thames, Buckingham Palace, The Mall, Whitehall with 10 Downing Street, Trafalgar Square and Houses of Parliament, and Big Ben were on our bucket list of "must see" places. The children seemed enthralled by it all; Gosia and I had a fun time. The streets were busy and narrow in certain places. The cars were close to the curb, and drivers were aggressive. I was once inches (or centimeters) from being clipped by an oncoming car. Pedestrians must protect themselves and be careful using the road, too.

There were indeed tall steel gates installed at the entrance to Downing Street. They sprung up in the 1970s when Margaret Thatcher was prime minister and there were tensions from the Irish Republican Army and other sources.

We departed from Heathrow Airport to Warsaw to be briefly with the family in Puławy. We planned another quick trip to the seaside, including Gdańsk this time, and then Białogóra and Kraków, as usual. In Gdańsk we rented a B&B in a historic tenement in the main town near the Motława River wharf. We strolled the Long Lane (*Ulica Długa*) from the Golden Gate (*Złota Brama*) to the Long Market (*Długi Targ*) and the Green Gate (*Zielona Brama*). I was selfish when Gosia wanted to buy souvenirs or desserts. I did not want to participate and share money with her. The lack of generosity on my part contributed to the weakening of our marriage.

In Białogóra we rented a plywood house on the campground

instead of a tent as before. Otherwise, the beach and the Baltic Sea were refreshing, relaxing, and invigorating. Jogging by the seashore or bodysurfing, when there is a high tide creating waves, are matchless in terms of fun, health benefits, and a sense of wellness that flows from physical accomplishment.

We flew to Minneapolis via Amsterdam on KLM-Northwest and from there drove back to Bismarck in our Suburban.

2.

The third winter in Bismarck was also very harsh. We saw that the Diamante was "wearing out" slowly and could not negotiate all the snowy and icy streets and hills in Bismarck. Its front-wheel drive was adequate but not perfect, and we traded it in the spring of 1997 for the green Oldsmobile Bravada. Rugged all-wheel-drive SUVs made more sense in North Dakota.

There was a big snowstorm in April 1997, with over a foot of snowfall. Even in an SUV, it was difficult to drive in the city, at least in the morning hours and in the immediate aftermath of the storm. I was on call that day and received a page from the hospital. A patient had a dangerously slow heart rate, and since no other causes could explain the situation, the decision was to insert a permanent pacemaker. I decided to walk to the hospital since we lived close and I did not want to waste time and energy clearing the driveway, which would have delayed everything. I made it to the hospital in less than fifteen minutes. The entire team arrived shortly after, and the patient's procedure was successful. Looking back, I was reminded of "the good old times" when a doctor had to go to see patients on foot, in a horse-drawn cart, or by other simple means of transport. I should have drawn conclusions from this situation, namely that always having the newest model of a car is not what makes us a true progressor and enables us to serve. Unfortunately, the old habits die hard, and it may take almost our entire adult lives to understand that. At the very least we should have an attitude of patience while waiting for our reward, saving money, and taking care of the family first, and only after we have saved money by years of arduous work may we reward ourselves later in life.

In July Barbara and Patrick visited us in America. I welcomed them at the Minneapolis-St. Paul Airport, and we drove to Bismarck. We spent three to four days at home, enjoying good food, thanks to Gosia's cooking, but we also went out once to Caspar East 40 Steakhouse and Tavern Restaurant. It was then and remains now a popular destination. Since the 1990s, it has changed ownership and name twice and now operates as 40 Steak + Seafood.

We did not go to the Badlands with our Scottish family but explored the vicinity of Bismarck and Mandan, the state capitol and North Dakota Heritage Center, Custer's House, Kirkwood Mall, and the downtown area around the Cathedral of the Holy Spirit.

We then drove back to Chicago; Ania wanted to go with us. We took our time to visit Minneapolis and St. Paul first, focusing on downtown Minneapolis and the Mall of America. Gosia and I made a dozen visits with our children to camp Snoopy (currently Nickelodeon Universe) in the 1990s. Usually, these were weekend trips from Bismarck. Children had their share of fun at the Log Chute, rock-climbing wall, and various rides. This time our Scottish guests, Ania, and I took pictures at the Log Chute, while starting our descent down the water channel. We saw the cathedrals in Minneapolis and in St. Paul. Then there was a relaxing afternoon at the Minnesota Zoo in Apple Valley. One more leg of the trip remained to finish in Chicago to see the highlights of the largest Midwest city. We walked down Michigan Avenue to Lake Shore Drive and went to the top of the Willis Tower (then known as the Sears Tower). It was at that time the tallest building in the world(!), but Petronas Towers in Kuala Lumpur, Malaysia, would soon overtake it and hold this distinction until 2004.

We met with Przemek, who came to our hotel, and we enjoyed the indoor pool. After Barbara and Patrick took off from O'Hare to London, Ania and I visited Przemek at his high-rise apartment on North Sheridan Road. He had finished four years of an internal medicine residency and was into his third year of a hematology-oncology fellowship. As I was walking between the tall buildings in the Lake Shore Drive area to find the nearest Western Union (Ania stayed with Przemek), a big flowerpot suddenly crashed to the ground two or three inches away, narrowly missing the left side of my head. It must have fallen from a considerable height; it obeyed the laws of gravity.

The next morning, Ania and I drove back to Bismarck in our Suburban.

3.

In December 1997, we closed on the purchase of a home on Carriage Circle. It was in a pleasant cul-de-sac, and the children enjoyed the backyard, which was almost one acre, with a spruce tree in the middle. There were shrubs on the outer border and a picturesque ravine beyond the boundaries of the property and the brow of the hill, where cows and deer were seen frequently. I later bought a Craftsman 42-inch riding lawnmower and did what other homeowners do, namely mow their yard every seven to ten days during summer.

We flew to Columbia for Christmas, which fell on Thursday that year, and were back in Bismarck on December 26. I had to be on call the entire following weekend. Family time needs to be valued, especially for the children; it provides opportunities for bonding across the generations.

We moved in at the end of January 1998. We added the furniture over time, but everything was comfortable and functional from the beginning. The house was built in 1985, and we were the second owners. There were three floors and a mezzanine, which served as a living room and TV room. We added a half bath in the basement after a year. We updated the appliances in the kitchen, removed the old wallpaper, and repainted the inside of the house in 1999 and the outside in 2000. We exchanged carpets for wooden floors in the entrance and main area.

In 1998 Gosia was diagnosed with multiple sclerosis. A close friend of ours, an orthopedic surgeon, detected increased reflexes in the arms on the examination. Gosia's symptoms consisted only of slight neck discomfort and occasional headaches. Much earlier, in 1984, when we were still awaiting our first reunion, Gosia had written me a letter from Puławy in which she mentioned certain neurological and visual symptoms she was experiencing. Her headaches were more frequent and severe then and diagnosed as migraines. She'd had a neurological examination, which did not reveal definite problems, but CT (Computerized Tomography) or MRI (Magnetic Resonance Imaging) were not available yet. She took Tylenol for headaches from time to time.

The orthopedist requested a neurological visit. Another friend of ours completed the evaluation. A CT scan was indeed suggestive. Gosia had generalized weakness for twenty-four to forty-eight hours and stayed in the hospital for three days. She had a spinal tap and later the MRI to confirm the diagnosis. Of course, this changed our lives. We tried to stay positive, use supportive treatment, and maintain a regular, healthy lifestyle that included taking vitamins and supplements. There was a medication called Avonex (interferon beta 1a), which had been available in the US since 1996, and Gosia's neurologist prescribed it after discussing everything in detail.

We already had a little cocker spaniel named Toby at home by then, and during Gosia's absence I took care of him and the house and did the necessary cleaning to keep the situation from getting out of control. There was a Good Samaritan lady from school who brought warm meals for the children. Somehow, we survived those bleak moments.

Gosia's response to the medications was good. There were no noticeable symptoms in the next weeks, and we even managed to go to Orlando/Kissimmee to visit Disneyworld in March. The theme parks were impressive: The Magic Kingdom, Epcot Center, and Disney's Hollywood Studios, with its breathtaking big-screen motion views of the six largest countries in the world. I appreciated Gosia's toughness and devotion to the family.

In late June and early July, we managed to go to the Polish seaside again.

Another five or six days in Białogóra were refreshing, as always. This time we rented two rooms in a brick house. There was a seafood restaurant in the village, which Alek called "a greasy food store," but we tried to make healthy choices as much as possible. There was a TV set there, on which we watched the final stages of the FIFA World Cup; France won by beating Brazil 3:0 in the final.

We returned to Bismarck without difficulty.

At the end of the year, we traded the Suburban for a '98 black Lincoln Navigator and the green Bravada for a coffee-colored '98 Bravada. I was still into having the newest model and the most current styling (which soon became dated).

4.

Another Christmas and New Year holiday season went fast, and the year 1999, the penultimate year of the twentieth century, started on a sad note. On January 3, Alek's ninth birthday, we received news of Gosia's mother's passing. Nina had been ill for the previous two years.

Gosia had another bout of generalized weakness, undoubtedly precipitated by stress. She did not go to the hospital but received intravenous corticosteroids as an outpatient and felt better after a few days.

I immediately purchased a plane ticket at a bereavement fare on KLM-Northwest Airline and flew through Minneapolis and Amsterdam to Warsaw. The funeral Mass and burial took place in Lublin, at the Lipowa Street Cemetery. I met more members of Gosia's family for the first time.

I stayed at my in-laws' home in Puławy. It was very cold. The time change and difference in diet caused me physical difficulties the first night and the second day. I found a book about the history of the Soviet Union and Stalin's political oppression in Soviet Russia in the 1930s and read it as a criminal thriller novel for the second or third time.

The first few weeks after returning home were mournful, but we had to continue with our duties. We invited Gosia's father, Ludwik, and brother, Bogdan, to visit us in the summer. They came in June to Minneapolis-St. Paul, and we drove to Bismarck. We did our best to relax, visiting the local attractions and watching the NBA Finals of the shortened 1988–1999 season. The San Antonio Spurs were the winners over the New York Knicks.

We then went to see the tourist attractions of western North Dakota and South Dakota, this time including the Medora Musical with its tasty pitchfork fondue. We explored Mount Rushmore and the Crazy Horse Memorial as a group of seven people.

The stories of the Borglum family and the Korczak Ziółkowski family run parallel. Korczak's ambition and independent spirit led him to become the author and sculptor of the Crazy Horse Memorial after he could not resolve the position of sculptor's assistant with Gutzon's son, Lincoln Borglum.

We returned to Bismarck, driving through the prairies of the Dakotas, and the time came to say goodbye again. We bought gifts for our Polish family; Gosia and I bought a medical album for Robert, Bogdan's son. He was already showing interest in studying medicine. Ludwik and Bogdan boarded the plane in Minneapolis-St. Paul.

In June, Ania finished seventh grade, Adam second, and Alek first. Adam received his First Holy Communion in April at the Cathedral of the Holy Spirit where we were the parishioners.

I had an invitation to attend a Mayo Clinic cardiology meeting in Napa Valley, and we decided to take off in our black Lincoln Navigator to see the Rockies, the Sierra Nevada range, and the diverse geography of Nevada and California. We stopped the first night in Chugwater, Wyoming, a one-of-a-kind, almost otherworldly place. The beds were comfortable in a roadside motel, and the burgers were big, nutritious, and tasty. The second day we drove to Winnemuca, Nevada, and likewise had a good night's rest. The third day we arrived in Napa in mid-afternoon. We stayed at the Silverado Resort and Spa. The meetings ended at noon; we used the remaining afternoon time for sightseeing and wine tasting. William Hill Estate Winery was the closest to the hotel; the Rutherford Hill Winery and Francis Ford Coppola Wineries were not far away.

The meetings finished on Sunday, and we drove to San Francisco, staying at a downtown Hyatt Hotel for the night. The next day we visited Fisherman's Wharf and dined on seafood at one of the restaurants at Pier 31.

Then we drove down to Los Angeles to visit my brother Przemek and Kasia. They lived at the Holly Street Apartments at that time, in a spacious, comfortable two-bedroom unit on the upper floor. Our hosts pitched the tent on the patio for the children; Gosia and I had a comfortable guest bedroom.

We had an enjoyable time, sampled a variety of foods, and drove to Disneyland Park and Resort in Anaheim. The rides and the attractions were superb, but they did not entirely overshadow those of Disneyworld in Orlando.

The return trip led us through Las Vegas, with a stop for lunch at Denny's restaurant at Las Vegas Boulevard, Denver, eastern Wyoming, and Spearfish, South Dakota. The drive was long; it took three days again, but the views of the mountains, rivers, and human settlements alongside the roads gave us the proper notion of the vastness and the beauty of America.

5.

The fall of 1999 was filled with events and constant changes. I was barreling toward my fortieth birthday in December; Gosia had marked hers earlier that year. There was a scare of Y2K on the horizon. Computer specialists feared that when the clocks struck midnight on January 1, 2000, affected computers would be using an incorrect date and thus fail to operate properly unless the software was updated or replaced. Computers turned out to be fine.

I had a "slow go" approach to computers at first and did not look at them much in the years 1994–1996. Then the prevailing way of doing business made it inevitable, and I kept up with the developments.

At that time, I had a foreboding to prepare myself for changes in life in the next year or two. With the experience gained, I thought that new challenges and professional paths would open.

In July I was elected fellow of the American College of Physicians.

In August, toward the end of the summer, we bought a sport boat, a Sea Ray Sundeck 210. Also, we bought two units of personal watercraft—a three-seat and a two-seat jet ski Sea Doo. We immediately started enjoying them on the Missouri River and at Lake Sakakawea, fifty miles north of Bismarck. Summer ended quickly, and we prepared our boat and watercraft for the winter.

In September I flew to Poland for six days, met with my friend Rysiek in Gdańsk and met with the persons from Mr. Lech Wałęsa's entourage to try to lay the groundwork for a visit with the whole family next year at his office at the Brama Ulicy Długiej (Golden Gate or *Langgasser Tor* in German). The details of the visit and its results were disheartening, and I only had myself to blame for this outcome. In retrospect I was a poseur exposing myself to false friends, to various temptations and distractions. Everything went well with Rysiek, but not so with other newly minted acquaintances.

My fortieth birthday was a memorable day. We invited friends and coworkers from the hospital, and it was truly an American-style party at our house. I received words of encouragement and broad support from personnel if I were to pursue a leadership position in the department of cardiology, but I felt an inside tension. With Gosia's illness in the background, I feared that our mutual bond was eroding. Important decisions in life require unity. But for that night our home was filled with friendly conversations, and the food cooked by Gosia added tremendously to the overall good atmosphere.

6.

In January 2000, I was appointed clinical associate professor of medicine at the University of North Dakota. We planned to go to Italy again in the summer. It was a Jubilee Year, officially held from Christmas Eve (December 24) 1999 to Epiphany (January 6) 2001.

Ania received the Sacrament of Confirmation in April (taking the confirmand's name of Lucy), and Alek received First Holy Communion later in the month. We had a special dinner at home, but I did not spend enough time with Alek to encourage him to reflect on the meaning of this event, lacking sufficient skill to be his guide in Catholic religion at that time. Adam had an innate religious sense, and we had some good discussions from time to time when he was thirteen or fourteen. One of these topics concerned Sedevacantism, a movement which holds that since October 1958, the occupiers of the Holy See have not been valid popes due to their espousal of many heresies.

I went to Rochester, Minnesota, to attend a weekend-long cardiology board review course. The course was intense and excellent. Mayo Clinic courses always provided a necessary boost of information and confidence and allowed for some high-quality professional networking.

By then we had traded our black Lincoln Navigator for a beige '00 Navigator with higher horsepower and our coffee-colored Bravada for a light green '00 Mercury Mountaineer. Both of these vehicles were strong enough to pull our boats and watercrafts.

We made plans to fly to Europe in mid-June to start from Munich. This time we boarded the plane in Bismarck, not adding time and mileage to drive to Minneapolis-St. Paul or Chicago. We finally became more conscious of time and convenience. Two connections, in Minneapolis-St.

Paul and in Amsterdam, delivered us to Munich.

The first night we quickly checked into Holiday Inn in the City Centre. The family needed rest. I made an effort to go for a walk to see as much of the old town as possible; the *Marienplatz* with the Column of Mary, the New City Hall, the *Frauenkirche* (Church of Our Lady, serving as the cathedral of the Archdiocese of Munich and Freising), and St. Peter's Church, the oldest recorded parish church in Munich.

The next morning, rested enough, we set off to Milan in Italy. We first drove on an autobahn, which is known for its liberal speed limits. (There are "suggested" speed limits of 80 mph, but in practice, drivers are free to go as fast as they want in derestricted sections of the autobahns.) We kept the speed of around 100 mph and passed trucks and slower cars, but frequently powerful and modern Mercedes, BMWs, and Porsches whizzed by on our left.

We chose to go through the eastern part of Switzerland to enjoy the views of the Swiss Alps. We stopped at a real alpine Swiss chalet and had hot chocolate and a snack consisting of a bagel and a pretzel.

There were truly breathtaking panoramas on our way to the Swiss-Italian border with little or no passport control at the border crossings. The European Union has been fully in place since its inception in 1993. At that time, I still had illusions about its positive role.

7.

We arrived in Milan in the evening. Milan is the capital of Lombardy. The distance between Munich and Milan is 350 miles (540 kilometers). We checked in to one of the Best Western Hotels. It was easy to reach the *Duomo di Milano*, or Milan Cathedral, with the Gold Statue of *Madonnina* (Little Madonna) on top of the cathedral.

The interior of the cathedral's architecture and art reflect almost six centuries of construction, from 1386 to the completion of the final details in 1965. There is a statue of St. Bartholomew Flayed and the tomb, among others, of recently beatified Cardinal Alfredo Ildefonso Schuster, a Benedictine monk and a promoter of liturgical piety who lived from 1870 to 1954.

Mark Twain visited Milan in the summer of 1867 and dedicated chapter 18 of his travel book, *Innocents Abroad*, to Milan Cathedral. He wrote about this supernaturally inspired treasure of human spirit and culture with glowing admiration.

There is an opulent shopping district next to the cathedral called *Galleria Vittorio Emanuele* II, which we briefly perused. A two-mile walk took us to the Church of *Santa Maria delle Grazie* with Leonardo da Vinci's (1452–1519) "The Last Supper." The mural painting is in the refectory of the church and is Leonardo's most famous masterpiece alongside the Mona Lisa, and one of the Western world's most recognizable paintings and celebrated works.

The painting sustained heavy damage in its five hundred-year history. During the French Revolution and the Napoleonic wars, the anticlerical troops used the refectory as an armory and stable, threw stones at the painting, and climbed up the ladders to scratch out the Apostles' eyes. During World War II, allied bombing did further damage. The restorations in 1970s and 1990s did not entirely reverse the structural losses.

Then a fifteen-minute stroll brought us to Sempione Park, a one hundred-acre public space. At the edge of the park lies Sforza's Castle, a towering brick façade built as a fortress in the fourteenth century.

The famous Giuseppe Meazza Stadium (San Siro) is about eight miles west from this area, a fifteen- to twenty-minute ride by car or metro. It is a venue of the famous "Derby della Madonnina," a football match between the two prominent Milanese clubs, Inter Milan and A.C. Milan.

From Milan we reached Florence, a distance of 195 miles (315 kilometers). Florence is the capital of Tuscany. We stayed at the Hotel Cavour near the Duomo (Florence Cathedral). Count Camillo Cavour was an Italian politician, one of the leading figures in the movement toward Italian unification in the nineteenth century (Risorgimento), a Freemason.

The hotel was good and comfortable, but it was not universally nonsmoking inside. We ended up in the room with the odor of previous cigarette use, despite requesting nonsmoking. My Italian was not much better than the hotel clerk's English; hence we did not go far in our discussion and took the room. Gosia and the children were more tranquil about it than I, and the air improved quickly.

Well rested, we walked to visit the cathedral. Its official name in Italian is Cattedrale di Santa Maria del Fiore (Cathedral of Saint Mary of the Flower). Filippo Brunelleschi (1377–1446) engineered the dome, which remains the largest brick dome ever constructed. He was the founding father of Renaissance architecture, a designer and sculptor who received the first patent in the Western world in 1421 for a crane system for shipping and transporting marble.

The exterior of the basilica has marble panels in shades of green and pink, bordered by white, and has an elaborate nineteenth-century façade.

The interior of the cathedral is austere. Baptistery of St. John is an octagonal building next to the cathedral. An octagon in Christian symbolism represents Jesus' Resurrection and eternity ("the eighth day"). The third building that makes up the Florence Cathedral complex is Giotto's Campanile, a bell tower. It has rich sculptural decorations and polychromic marble encrustations.

We reached Piazza della Signoria with the statue of David by Michelangelo Buonarroti (1475–1564). The entrance to the Uffizi Gallery is nearby. It is one of the largest and best-known museums in the world and holds a collection of priceless works from the period of the Italian Renaissance.

The river Arno cuts through the old part of the city. The most famous bridge is the Old Bridge (Ponte Vecchio), who's most striking feature is the multitude of shops built upon its edges, held up by stilts.

From Florence we reached Assisi, the place of Saint Francis. It is only 110 miles (174 kilometers) in the southeastern direction by Autostrada A1/E35.

In Assisi, our destination was the Basilica of Saint Francis, which divides into the Upper and the Lower Basilica. In the crypt there is a burial place of the founder of the Franciscan Order. We did not reach the Portiuncula this time, a small church within the Basilica of St. Mary of the Angels where St. Francis died and where the Franciscan movement started. The name of the Basilica served the Franciscan missionaries as the name of the settlement, which became Los Angeles in California. I still had memories from the visit in 1987.

In Rome, we checked into the Residenza Paolo VI Hotel. It was comfortable, with an excellent restaurant that served authentic, tasty Italian pastas with tomato and marinara sauces (salsa marinara and salsa di pomodoro). Our waiters' smiles and sense of humor were infectious; they especially seemed to like Alek, who enjoyed the experience very much.

The next day started with the tour of St. Peter's Basilica. On our trip we rarely relied on professional guides but instead bought printed materials to learn about the historic and religious landmarks.

We found out that women were not allowed inside the Basilica with their shoulders uncovered, and we had to go back to the stores around St. Peter's Square to buy Gosia a scarf that fulfilled the requirements of proper modesty. It was an omission on our part; we should have prepared ourselves better.

It is impossible to embrace the Basilica in one vision and one single memory. Besides the main altar and the ancient bronze statue of St. Peter, which has his right toes worn down by the centuries of pilgrims who traditionally touch the foot, we immediately call to mind Michelangelo's Pieta, located just to the right of the entrance, between the holy door and the altar of Saint Sebastian. (In 1972 the statue was vandalized by a disturbed man but restored fully and placed behind the bulletproof acrylic glass panel.)

Also, we paid a visit to the tomb of Pope St. Pius X, whose incorrupt body lies in a glass coffin, his face covered with a bronze mask.

After seeing the Sistine Chapel (the site of conclave when a new pope is elected, this time more hushed than on our previous visit nineteen years ago), with Michelangelo's ceiling frescoes, including "The Creation of Adam" and "The Last Judgment," which covers the altar wall, we proceeded to the Vatican Museums. These house 54 rooms with priceless art collections, paintings, and Roman objects, accumulated by the popes over the centuries. One recognizes in this place the brevity of life and the larger context in which the drama of human life is taking place. One is looking for order, for a meaning beyond the immediate material reality, to sublimate human aspirations to touch the divine.

From there, the Castle of the Holy Angel (Castel Sant'Angelo) is one of the closest important sites to visit. It was a mausoleum for Emperor Hadrian in the second century. After Archangel Michael appeared here in 590 AD and ended a plague, Pope Pius II had a large bronze statue of the angels placed on top of the castle. The castle was part of Rome's defenses and offered a place where the popes could shelter, including a tunnel leading to it from the Vatican. Pope Clement VII took refuge in the castle for six months during the siege of Rome by the mutinous forces of Emperor Charles V in 1527.

The next day took us to the Piazza Navona, which is an elongated square, as it served as a Roman athletics' stadium, with the Fountain of the Four Rivers (Fontana dei Quattro Fiumi) in the center. It was designed in 1651 by Gian Lorenzo Bernini, who was also the sculptor of the Colonnade at St. Peter's Square, for Pope Innocent X. The rivers represent four major rivers of the four continents: Nile in Africa, Danube in Europe, the Ganges in Asia, and Rio de la Plata in the Americas, through which papal authority had spread. Then the Spanish Steps and the Trevi Fountain with the god of the sea Neptune on his chariot are the tourist spots not to be omitted. From there it is close to the Pantheon, the oldest building in the world that is still in use today. It was built in

125 by Emperor Hadrian and served as a temple to all Roman gods. It became a Catholic Church in 609 as Basilica of St. Mary and the Martyrs under Pope St. Boniface IV.

The Roman Forum (Forum Romanum) was a center of day-to-day life in Rome, the site of triumphal processions, elections, public speeches, criminal trials, and gladiatorial matches. Today it is a sprawling ruin of architectural fragments and archeological excavations. Among the surviving structures are Tarpeian Rock (site of executions), Temple of Saturn, Temple of Vespasian, and Titus. The Colosseum is further east; we visited it with awe, imagining the audience of 60,000 to 80,000 people participating in gladiatorial contests and public spectacles, including animal hunts, executions, enactments of land battles, and sea battles. Early Christians were persecuted for their refusal to worship the emperor and the Roman gods and were fed to half-starved lions, burned alive, and hacked to death, many embracing martyrdom with courage.

Southeast of the Colosseum is the Old Appian Way (Via Appia Antica), about 4 miles (7 km) away. We covered it on foot, resting and having a snack, gelato (ice cream), and a lemonade in a pizzeria or trattoria along the way. We relied sometimes on public transportation as driving in a rented car in the city proved difficult.

The Old Appian Way is fascinating, housing the Catacombs of San Sebastiano and San Callisto, site of burial of the early Christians. There is a small church of Domine Quo Vadis, with the story described in the apocryphal Acts of Peter and immortalized in the Nobel Prize-winning novel, *Quo Vadis*, written by Henryk Sienkiewicz in 1896 and adapted for screen and made into an epic Hollywood production in 1951. It shows the scene when Christ met Peter as the latter was fleeing Rome. Peter asked Christ, "Lord, where are you going?" (*"Domine, quo vadis?"*) To which Christ replied, "I go to Rome to be crucified a second time" (*"Eo Romam iterum crucifigi"*).

The church dates to at least the ninth century when it was known as Santa Maria in Palmis. In the seventeenth century the church was rebuilt and renamed Domine Quo Vadis. The church is a home to a marble slab (today a copy of the original, which is kept in the nearby Basilica of San Sebastiano), which bears the imprint of a pair of feet, held to be a miraculous sign left by Jesus. It is to these footprints (*palmis*) that the original name of the church refers.

We spent the last days in Rome closer to the city center. The visit to Rome would not be complete without a walk to the city center to Piazza Venezia. Via dei Fori Imperiali connects the Piazza (Square) with the Colosseum. The square is at the foot of the Capitoline Hill and next to Trajan's Forum. On the side of the square is the Tomb of the Unknown Soldier in the Altar of the Fatherland (Altare della Patria), a monument to Victor Emmanuel II (1820–1878), the first king of Italy.

Our stay in Rome was ending. We enjoyed the time and everything this great city, a cradle of the Western civilization, had to offer. However, I had a gnawing feeling that Gosia and I were not drawing closer spiritually and mentally; if anything, we were getting more distant. Things that were happening on "autopilot" in the previous twenty years were not so anymore; they now required more mutual openness, cultivation, discussion, and prayer, which was missing. I could not provide a good example of a daily prayer for my wife and children, expecting that things would always work out in the future as they had in the past. It did not turn out to be quite so simple.

The last afternoon and evening we spent soaking up the views, feeling the winds coming from the Mediterranean Sea and the Roman sun. We tossed a coin in the Trevi Fountain, to signify that we hoped to return to Rome again. The custom of tossing coins in the fountains started there.

8.

The next morning we took a trip to the southeast of Italy from the region of Lazio, where Rome is located, through the regions of Campania,

Basilicata, and Puglia with its capital, Bari.

Before reaching Bari, we stopped in Pompeii, in Campania, near the coast of the Bay of Naples. Once a thriving city, it was buried along with Herculaneum and the surrounding villas under meters of ash and pumice after the eruption of Mount Vesuvius in 79 AD. It is now an archeological site. Major excavations were done prior to 1960 and left parts of the city in decay. They were later limited to targeted areas. There is a well-preserved Villa of the Mysteries in the city with the frescoes, along with the ancient temples and the reconstructed streets, which we saw from the inside out.

Pompei is associated with the Shrine of the Blessed Virgin of the Rosary, commissioned in 1901 by Bartolo Longo, a lawyer and a former Satanist priest who converted to the Catholic faith, became a third order Dominican, and dedicated his life to the Rosary and the Virgin Mary. There is a Basilica of St. Nicholas in Bari (a prototype of Santa Claus), which is an important pilgrimage destination for Roman Catholics and Orthodox Christians. In the Basilica there is a tomb of St. Nicholas of Myra, which houses his relics and of the Queen of Poland Bona Sforza, second wife of King Sigismund the Old, and a Duchess of Bari in her own right.

We passed through the city of Bari very quickly and did not visit the Shrine in Pompeii or the Basilica in Bari. We boarded a ferry to Igoumenitsa in Greece. Our rented Chrysler was in the cargo space below, and we decided to upgrade our initially purchased deck seats to two inside cabins with comfortable cots.

The sea voyage took about twelve hours to cross the Ionian Sea, 250 nautical miles. Disembarking from the ferry was quick, and we took the main road to Athens, which was 290 miles (470 km) southeast. We did not cross the Gulf of Corinth, which separates Central Greece from the Peloponnese. The only strip of land that connects the two is the Isthmus of Corinth. Since 1893 the Corinth Canal has run through the 6.3-kilometer isthmus, effectively making the Peloponnese an island.

We arrived at the city of Athens from the north and booked into the Crowne Plaza Hotel, three miles (5 kilometers) from the Acropolis, which we promptly visited the next morning, starting our Athenian experience. The Acropolis is an ancient citadel on a rocky outcrop containing ancient buildings, the most famous being the Parthenon, the former temple dedicated to the goddess Athena during the fifth century BC. Its sculptures remain the enduring symbols of Ancient Greece, democracy, and Western civilization. It is a hill of 512 feet (156 meters), and there is no lift. It means that reaching the Acropolis requires stamina and physical preparedness.

Soon after we directed our steps to the Areopagus (Mars Hill) where the Apostle Paul preached his famous sermon in 51 AD. This sermon is recounted in the Acts of the Apostles 17:24–31. The Athenians used an altar with the inscription, "TO AN UNKNOWN GOD." Therefore, what the Athenians worshipped in ignorance, Paul could proclaim to them. "The God who made the world and everything that is in it, since He is Lord of heaven and earth, does not dwell in temples made by hands, nor is he served by human hands, since He himself gives to all people life and breath and all things; [. . .] He is not far from each one of us, for in Him we live and move and exist. [. . .] Each person is His offspring, so there is no person or sphere outside of His concern." We had seen the brass plaque commemorating Apostle Paul's sermon twenty centuries ago on the hillside.

Athens is surrounded by waters of the Gulf of Corinth from the Ionian Sea in the west, the Saronic Gulf of the Aegean Sea east of the Isthmus of Corinth, and the Gulf of Evoikos. The island of Patmos where Apostle John had his vision resulting in authoring the last book of the Sacred Scripture, the Book of Revelation (Apocalypse), is on the Aegean Sea, two hundred miles miles east of Athens. We did not go to Patmos or to the western coast of Anatolia in Turkey, but we obviously felt the touch and inspiration of history in Athens.

We breathed the refreshing summer air and sampled traditional

Greek food, Moussaka (eggplant or potato-based dish with meat), Pita (flatbread) Spanakopita (spinach pie), Tzatziki (traditional sauces), and Souvlaki (meat-on-a-skewer). The time came quickly to say goodbye to the City of Wisdom (one of the nicknames of the Greek capital) and head back to Italy, a country that spanned the territory of and evolved from ancient Rome, the originator of the Western legal system.

The final leg of our Mediterranean trip awaited us, 505 miles (815 kilometers) north of Venice. The drive was smooth and uneventful. After crossing the Liberty Bridge (Ponte della Liberta) that connects the mainland part of the city to its historic center surrounded by water, one must park the car at the Piazzale Roma and take a water taxi or walk to get close to St. Mark's Square (Piazza San Marco). Venice is built on 118 islands in a lagoon in the Adriatic Sea. They are separated by canals and linked by over four hundred bridges.

We checked in at Hotel Mercurio, about a half mile away from the center of Venice. We wasted no time in proceeding to St. Mark's Square and entered St. Mark's Basilica. It holds the relics of the Evangelist, who is the patron saint of the city.

The basilica is built in the Byzantine, Romanesque, and Gothic style. The present structure is the third church, begun in 1063 to express Venice's growing consciousness and pride. Prior to the fall of the republic of Venice in 1797, it was a chapel of the Doge (chief magistrate and leader of the Republic of Venice). The interior of the basilica has Byzantine (Eastern) and Renaissance influences. The main altar is located within the apse (a semicircular protruding part of the building). The mosaic of Christ Pantocrator is in the semi-dome of the apse. Below are late-eleventh century mosaics that portray Saint Nicholas of Myra (the same saint whose relics are in Bari), Saint Peter, Saint Mark, and Saint Hermagoras of Aquilea. Over the high altar in the eastern crossarm is the Dome of Immanuel ("God with us"). An extensive cycle narrating the Life of Christ covers the interior of the basilica. The eastern vault covers the major events of infancy (Annunciation, Adoration of the

Magi, Presentation in the Temple), and the western vault depicts the events of the Passion, Crucifixion and Resurrection.

The Dome of the Ascension occupies the central position.

The remainder of St. Mark's Square with the Bell Tower of St. Mark's Basilica (Campanile di San Marco), the Doge Palace, and the Library of Saint Mark (Biblioteca Marciana) were memorable sites, the whole complex having served as a backdrop for several spy-action movies.

After this experience, I had a feeling that the remainder of the city, however magnificent, was almost anticlimactic. We went to the glass factory in Murano and saw the various production stages of the famous Murano glass. We bought a small souvenir, which was unfortunately lost when we left Bismarck.

We could not resist the ride in the gondola around the city along the canals, including, of course, the Grand Canal and the Rialto Bridge (Ponte di Rialto), the oldest of all the bridges of Venice.

After the last evening meal consisting of super tasty pizza, spaghetti, and tagliolini noodles with risotto and small fish from the lagoon waters, we repaired for the night to our hotel to get ready for the drive the next day to Vienna, Austria.

The distance from Venice to Vienna is 362 miles (584 kilometers) in the northeastern direction, and the drive was smooth and quick. There was no slowing down at the Italian-Austrian border.

We had just two days in Vienna. We saw the Hofburg Palace from the outside (still the largest former imperial palace in the world by floor area at 2.6 million square feet, or about 240,000 square meters) and St. Stephen's Cathedral. Gosia and I retraced with our children where we had once trod nineteen years earlier. Schonbrunn ("beautiful spring") Palace, the summer residence of the Habsburg rulers, is about four miles from the city center; we had to leave it out again.

We just had one day to return our rental car and go to the Central Station (Hauptbahnhof). The train to Kraków during the day was comfortable and inexpensive (around 20 Euros for an adult), with a pleasant restaurant car. We arrived in Kraków in the afternoon and visited my parents for the evening. Their apartment on the fourth floor of a tenement house served as a gathering place for the family. They were still living in Columbia, Missouri, but were spending summers in Kraków.

We went to Puławy the next day and from there once again to the Polish seaside.

This time we stayed for five days at the Hotel Gdynia (the northernmost city in the tri-city metropolitan area of Gdańsk, Sopot, and Gdynia, forming a row on the coastline of the Gdańsk Bay). Ania, Adam, and Alek appreciated a structured playground and sandpit by the hotel. Swimming in the Gdańsk Bay was not as great as in the "open" Baltic Sea.

I wanted to meet the former Polish president Lech Wałęsa, whom I thought played a positive role in the transformation in Poland and elsewhere in Europe in the 1980s and 1990s. Afterward he had suffered a huge loss of popularity and was constantly attacked in the media and dragged through courts (while filing his own countersuits) with the accusations of "collaborating with the secret police instead of being an honorable leader of Solidarity," as he had always presented himself. I did not believe these accusations. In every totalitarian system (or even a nominally free political system), a citizen must come at times into contact with law enforcement, security services, and police, especially if such person is politically active and occupies a position of prominence. It is not surprising that such figures will be approached, pressured, or even intimidated. Signing a document that "one will respect the current law" does not represent a betrayal of one's ideals or one's companions.

Of course, every political figure's time in the limelight is limited, and Wałęsa was perceived in the rearview mirror, as a leader who contributed much in the past but who should now enjoy his retirement. The reason for my pursuing contact with Mr. Wałęsa was that I had briefly harbored a fantasy of trying to become his political adviser and promote an idea of European collaboration based on the elements of Polish Catholicism, creating a counterbalance to the secular program of the European Union and influencing Russia. I also liked the idea of contesting the status of the Kaliningrad region incorporated into the Soviet Russia as an exclave in 1945. It historically belonged to Germany, wedged in between Poland and Lithuania, just north of the Warmia-Masuria Voivodeship. Wałęsa blurted it out in one of his speeches in the 1990s. I am glad that my musings had no chance of becoming a reality, and now, years later, the events had corrected my previous illusions and assessment of people. One must remain level-headed in life.

Gosia did not want to meet with Mr. Wałęsa, and I was caught between "a rock and a hard place." Once the former president's entourage found out that my family was not enthusiastic, Mr. Wałęsa begged himself out of the meeting, and my dreams lay in ruins. I left a courtesy note for Mr. Wałęsa, acknowledging his role in achieving a new, more just system in Poland after 1989, signing it with my name "and family."

The next day we met with his coworkers in the Grand Hotel in Sopot for lunch to "grasp at straws" one last time to continue our relationship, but there was an empty feeling. We had time to walk the Molo (Pier) in Orłowo and the main artery in the city, St. John's (Świętojańska) Street, with an excellent bookstore nearby. I bought three thick volumes recounting the life and ministry of Cardinal Wyszyński. Gosia bought a novel for herself, and the children also purchased illustrated books about Poland. (Adam always had the most interest in speaking Polish, and he remains perfectly proficient in it today. Ania and Alek also have good knowledge of the language.)

I had to return to Bismarck, having been gone for almost six weeks, and prepared myself to make up for the long time off. Gosia and the children stayed in Europe for two more weeks. Ania and Adam went to England, Scotland, and Ireland with their paternal grandparents. Gosia and Alek stayed in Puławy with Gosia's family.

I had the opportunity to visit Denny Newell for a social meeting and a boat ride on Lake Minnetonka in August with a group of his friends. It was a pleasant evening with a meal and conversation over a glass of beer or wine. Denny had a classic 1934 Mer-Na boat, beautifully restored, with a modern engine and navigation system. I later visited Denny and his wife Mary again in December after Christmas.

9.

The family returned to Bismarck in late August. In September my parents and my mother's youngest sister, Basia, came to visit us in Bismarck. We had an enjoyable time at Sertoma Park by the Missouri River and a family dinner at Caspar's East 40 Restaurant.

Around that time, we upgraded from the Sundeck boat to a Sea Ray Sundancer 300. It was a much larger vessel with a cabin downstairs that could sleep up to three to four people, and a toilet and shower. Adam and Alek enjoyed going with me to Lake Sakakawea, which we managed to do once or twice that year. Gosia and Ania were less inclined to go, for obvious reasons related to comfort and privacy, and, in Gosia's case, additionally because of the untoward effects on her underlying medical condition. We sold both Sea Doo personal watercrafts, but I purchased a Bombardier DS 650 ATV to take it on a trail from time to time.

Another detail that occupied my attention was a problem with five upper teeth. They had large fillings installed in childhood, which had finally cracked and needed root canal treatment. I never felt entirely comfortable with the root canals; they ached intermittently until twenty years later, when they were replaced with five implants in Sioux Falls, South Dakota. The implants provided truly excellent results and restoration of comfort. Dr. Aaron Aadland, Dr. Brent Henriksen, and their nursing and administrative teams showed great skill, professionalism, and cordiality.

Winter came and went, with the pleasant interlude of a visit with Denny and Mary at their house at Lake Minnetonka, which afforded splendid scenery and evening walks in cold temperatures.

The year 2001 brought substantial changes in my life and in our family life. I thought of seeking professional advancement within the structures of the hospital and had a discussion with the then-CEO of the hospital in January 2001. I already served on the Bylaws Committee but thought that I should pursue more administrative responsibilities, even at a cost of reduction in clinical involvement. The discussion did not result in harmonization of the positions, and I was given a green light to look for a position elsewhere. The CEO himself resigned as of March 31, and for a brief period I struggled with the decision of whether to apply for the vacated CEO position or continue to work predominantly as a clinician. I sensed that applying for a purely administrative position would be premature and that it would represent a departure from our previous structure of family life. I thought I would be tempted to look at my family too much in the rearview mirror and mentally drift apart from them. In February I went to New York City for a weekend to be a part of a meeting of Polish Americans with Lech Wałęsa, who was coming to give one of his post-presidency talks. It was good but more of a recap of previous events rather than an outline of a future political program. I posed a question after the talk to Mr. Wałęsa: "Why did you not win the second term in 1995 but lose to a post-Communist candidate?" There were gasps of surprise in the room. I did not register his answer.

In March I took a long weekend off and drove the Navigator from Bismarck to Jackson Hole, Wyoming, for three days of skiing. Jackson Hole is a part of Grand Teton National Park, which includes the major peaks of the Teton range. It is south of Yellowstone National Park.

Ania flew in from Bismarck a day later. The mountain was a skier's delight. There are thirteen lifts and 130 trails, including 50 percent that are expert level, 40 percent intermediate, and 10 percent beginner. With a 4,139-foot vertical drop, the mountain provides the most challenging ski conditions in the country. I skied down the double black runs, including Corbet's Couloir, Central Chute, and Pepi's Run (named after Austrian

Olympic athlete Josef "Pepi" Stiegler, who was an Olympic champion in slalom in 1964 in Innsbruck and later founded the Jackson Hole Ski School). Ania did very well on her snowboard on the difficult runs.

This was my first skiing trip in six years. I had not lost my zest for the sport, and the left knee injury sustained in Szczyrk thirty years earlier was not a factor, either physically or mentally. Ski equipment had improved exponentially in the thirty years, and the relatively stationary position of my knee while skiing did not cause any discomfort, as opposed to what I felt while running. Skiing is an aerobic, cardiovascular workout to a large degree, more akin to rowing or cycling, and it served me well in this phase of life. I was glad that our children picked it up to a degree.

Just after returning home, my former mentor and colleague Dr. Richard Schmaltz came to Bismarck and talked to the hospital administration and physicians, but I was notified about it late, and we did not have the opportunity to connect or exchange information. Dr. Schmaltz did not stay in Bismarck. We have not had any contact since, but I always remember him with great esteem.

I decided to bide my time with everything and continue as if "nothing had happened." While pondering independent practice as a long-term solution, I obtained a position as a cardiologist at Trinity Hospital in Minot, North Dakota, 110 miles north of Bismarck. This was meant to provide a financial foundation for a startup. The family home remained at Carriage Circle, the children continued with their school and religious education, and Gosia took care of the family. I rented a small apartment in Minot. Just before starting the assignment in Minot, I went to Cuba as a member of the People-to-People Ambassador Program. Established in 1956 by the President Dwight Eisenhower administration, it offered travel opportunities for middle and high school students. Adults and athletes also participated. This was one of the last years of operation before it converted into a for-profit company, which ceased operations in 2015.

I flew to Minneapolis-St. Paul and then to Miami and to Nassau, capital of the Bahamas. The group was already being assembled at Miami International Airport, and I met my fellow travelers, a group of twenty to twenty-five people. Two medical students (one male, one female) from the University of North Dakota and Mayo Clinic in Rochester, Minnesota, I knew already. In Nassau, on New Providence Island, I saw the Atlantis Resort from afar and the Queen's Staircase, which is located at Fort Fincastle Historic Complex. I walked on the pristine Cabbage Beach with its powdery white sand, palm trees that sway in the Caribbean breeze, and clear water that always looks inviting.

Nassau has its own unforgettable atmosphere and is a suitable location for filming spy and adventure movies.

The next day we flew to Havana on Bahamas Air since the US aircraft was not permitted to fly and land in the Cuban capital.

We checked into Hotel Melia, a five-star hotel between Fifth Avenue and the sea, in the Miramar business area. Melia is a Spanish hotel chain, the seventeenth biggest worldwide. The standard was high, and the food was outstanding. Our tour guide was a Cuban student with an excellent command of English and deep knowledge of the history and geography of his country of birth. We visited the Revolution Square (Plaza de la Revolucion) with the monument of the Cuban nationalist, poet, philosopher, translator, and publisher Jose Marti. On the other side of the square there was a mural of Ernesto Che Guevara (Argentinian Marxist, a major figure of the Cuban Revolution in 1959) on the Ministry of the Interior. The overall impression of the square was that of a drab, Communist reality. There were no stands with sodas, bagels, or cotton candy, no signs of entrepreneurship and "capitalist" activity. We later visited his mausoleum in Santa Clara, 180 miles (280 kilometers) southeast of Havana, but I perceived the leftist, revolutionary endeavors of people such as Fidel Castro, Ernesto Guevara, and many others as completely misguided, resulting in the loss of human life and economic opportunity.

I went several times to Mass at the Chapel of the Immaculate

(Capilla la Inmaculada), and it was consoling to see signs of faith, even in an officially atheist, Communist country. The congregation was small in the morning, but nothing was missing in the liturgical rite, even if I understood little to no Spanish at that time and had difficulty following the homily word-for-word.

We visited the state hospital in Havana, and surprisingly the physicians were able to display recent developments in the treatment of coronary artery disease with the newest catheters and stents. They had contacts with the hospitals in Mexico and Argentina.

Later, three of my closest companions on this trip and I went to a farewell dinner hosted for us by a Cuban couple. The meal consisted of a grilled fish (red snapper) and vegetables such as cucumber and tomato, as well as Cuban root crops such as taro and yuca. It was revealing to find out that the underground market in Cuba was thriving despite the empty shelves of the official state stores.

We went to a Cuban store that carried famous Cuban rum, such as Havana Club Seleccion de Maestros and Ron Cubay 11. Cuban rum is required to be aged at least twice, and optionally, even a third time. I was not interested in the cigars but bought a bottle of rum. It was strong; my face became flushed, and I had a "different" feeling in my joints. It was a continuation of the problem with elevated uric acid, which had started at Peacock Alley in Bismarck in the 1990s, and which would later manifest itself in achy joints due to a few bouts of gout. I made necessary dietary adjustments later than I should have and started taking a small dose of Allopurinol in 2007.

We visited the Ernest Hemingway Museum, a house called Finca Vigia (Lookout Farm) in the San Francisco de Paula Ward of Havana, built in 1886. The writer lived there in the 1940s and 1950s.

Our tourist group spent our final two days and two nights in Varadero, east of Havana. This is an internationally recognized destination with incredibly fine sandy beaches and warm, clear waters. The swimming was incomparable, very relaxing and rejuvenating. We returned to Miami via Nassau and from there to our respective destinations in the US.

In July I made a trip to Los Angeles where I visited my brother and sister-in-law again. Przemek's in-laws were visiting at the same time, and we had a pleasant, relaxing time, if only for the weekend. I did some pacemaker-related business on Thursday and Friday, talking with the representatives of St. Jude-Pacesetter company thanks to Denny's connections, and receiving updates on the recent technological developments. I flew back to Bismarck on Monday.

10.

The pay at Trinity Hospital represented substantial progress. I traded the Navigator for a beige Ford F-350 Super Duty 6.7 L diesel engine, which made me more confident pulling the big boat to lake Sakakawea. The Mountaineer remained the second vehicle.

On September 11, 2001, terrorist attacks on the World Trade Center shocked the world. I had planned to attend an educational interventional cardiology course in Atlanta, Georgia, in October, and even before the attacks, I'd wanted to drive the 1,550 miles in two days. I hoped to enjoy Ford Super Duty and visit my family in Hopkinsville, Kentucky (Barbara, the daughter of Grandfather Karol's brother Dolek, his wife Elwira, and her husband Marshall), as well as my friends from medical school, Timothy and Janice, who lived with their three children in Jackson, Tennessee.

I had not approached the course with my full attention at that juncture, letting go of this area of work and preparing for a different professional path. I felt that the period of interventional cardiology study and practice had come to an end.

In December 2001 we drove again to Jackson Hole. Since it was the time of Advent, we sang Christmas songs, from serious to humorous, including the famous "Grandma Got Run Over by a Reindeer." We must have gone over the refrain with Alek at least a hundred times.

The skiing vacation was refreshing; breathing fresh mountain air and working on cardiovascular fitness always paid dividends.

In March 2002 we drove to Jackson Hole for the third time, this time in a white 2002 Chevrolet Tahoe, for which the Navigator made room. (Ania received a bright red 2002 Chevrolet Cavalier at the time of our purchase of the Tahoe.) Ania flew in later in the day with her friend Erica. (Gosia and the boys stayed home this time.) Our parents and Przemek joined us three in Jackson for the weekend. Of the skiing vacations, I can only say that I wished each one of them had lasted a little longer.

At that time, our cocker spaniel, Toby, was having health problems, and I went with him twice to the University of Minnesota Veterinary Hospital. He broke a bone in his rear leg; it was pinned and treated aggressively, but it was not meant to be. He lost his ability to walk, and in April we grieved his departure.

After eight or nine months in Minot, it became apparent in February or March that my work there was not sustainable. I did not have enough connections in Minot (as opposed to Bismarck) but rather thought about opening my own office and adding an element of individual business risk to my activities. This became a source of major stress and disagreement with Gosia. She fretted about the path I was choosing and did not support it. It put an enormous test and strain on the marriage, and, in retrospect, it was the writing on the wall that our paths would separate in the future.

In May I attempted to pass the Interventional Cardiology Board examination in Minneapolis but missed it narrowly. I accepted it as the conclusion of this stage in my life and felt more unencumbered to pursue other interests and ideas in the medical field.

To conclude the political thread of the story, after the February 2001 meeting in New York, my interest in the person of Lech Wałęsa had waned. There was one more occasion to attend a meeting with the Nobel Peace Prize laureate in the fall of 2008 after he had a stent and a pacemaker-defibrillator implanted earlier at Houston Methodist DeBakey Heart and Vascular Center. This was one of his follow-up medical visits, and well-known political figures from Texas also delivered their addresses. The 41st US president, George H. W. Bush, gave the welcoming remarks but afterwards excused himself. Texas Congressman Charlie Wilson, of Operation Cyclone fame (a covert operation, which during the Carter and Reagan administrations supplied military equipment to the Afghan Mujahedeen during the Soviet Afghan War), otherwise known for his "flamboyant lifestyle," accompanied Mr. Wałęsa at the dais.

These two politicians had certain common themes in life. Both were engaged in "subversive" political activity, and both ended up with major medical problems, requiring heart surgeries. They used this time to thank the medical profession, in medical as well as political testimony, especially cardiologists and surgeons at the Houston Methodist Hospital. Mr. Wilson had a heart transplant in 2007 and died suddenly in 2010. Mr. Wałęsa lost his power of inspiration.

In retrospect, I look at my interest in politicians as a misguided effort and a waste of time. My conscience (God's voice, previously muffled) was giving me obvious signs that this was not the proper course to follow; I understood it belatedly. The price of my obstinacy and blindness was paid in the humiliations I had to endure in my body, mind, and soul. This all ended after I resolved to return to the right path. One must follow God unreservedly and not become dissipated in vain human pursuits.

The next morning, I went to Confession and Mass at Annunciation Church, which had a solemn and traditional atmosphere, even with the Novus Ordo Mass.

Chapter 6

CARDIOLOGY OFFICE AND CONTRACT WORK

1.

In May 2002 I returned to Bismarck. I was looking to open an independent medical office. A spacious office became available on Main Street, in the western part of Bismarck bordering Mandan. The views were excellent in the western direction, and there was ample sunlight in the afternoon hours. There were signs that this endeavor might be feasible, and that success may be achievable. Medcenter One Hospital, which I had previously worked in, granted me the privileges of performing cardiac catheterization, angioplasty, and stent procedures, as well as installing pacemakers.

I signed a three-year lease agreement with the owners of the building, with a month-to-month option afterwards. I purchased furniture, pictures, and paintings to decorate the walls and received others as gifts from my parents, family, and friends. A business service company assisted with setting up the practice management and medical billing software. The office was fitted with four computers, each destined to support various aspects of work: the administrative part and scheduling, patients' records, accounting, and support of echocardiography and other medical equipment.

Gosia was touchingly engaged in making things go forward. She managed phone calls, administrative duties, and even maintenance issues. After two or three weeks it became apparent that I would need a full-time administrative assistant; a person with professional experience applied for the position, and we signed a six-month contract. This was a very stressful time in our marriage and our family.

Soon thereafter, the person who attempted to work as a secretary resigned, but there were nervous moments with short-lived legal posturing between her and me. It all ended, and another person came to work as an administrative assistant. This person remained in her position until January 2005.

We acquired a Hewlett-Packard echocardiographic machine, and almost immediately the opportunity arose to participate in a screening program of the patients who previously took medications prescribed for weight loss: fenfluramine (Pondimin) and phentermine. This combination was known as fen-phen, and it was popular in the 1990s. Later, dexfenfluramine (Redux) was introduced. It was effective, but in 1997 two separate studies in the *New England Journal of Medicine* linked these drugs to cardiac problems such as valvular disease, primary pulmonary hypertension (PPH), and cardiac fibrosis. These problems affected one in three patients who took the drug. The manufacturer, Wyeth, was a subsidiary of the distributing company American Home Products. They were both involved in a class-action lawsuit settlement, which resulted in over $12 billion paid in damages and fees. Our office was selected to perform the screening of the eligible patients in North Dakota, and we were reimbursed for the echocardiogram test at a special rate. There were salaries to be paid to the technologists, but there was a "fair" profit for the office. This program lasted until the spring of 2003.

Gosia, the children, and I had planned to take time off in June, but we decided to split our journey so that I would visit the family in Poland and then in Edinburgh, Scotland, and Gloucestershire, England, in the last days of May and first days of June. Then I would fly to Lisbon, Portugal, where Gosia and the children would be waiting at the airport, having arrived there an hour earlier from Bismarck. This required planning and coordination. I spent four days in Poland first, then in Kraków, then in Warsaw, where I saw the last surviving sister of Grandfather Karol's, Aunt Maryla Staszewska, nee Nowosielska. Her son Paweł was away at that time, but we later met and got to know each other, spending time together in Warsaw in 2016. We discussed a possible trip to California and New Mexico on Facebook Messenger; this remained in the planning stages. Then I flew from Warsaw to Glasgow.

My brief visit to Edinburgh and King's Stanley in Gloucestershire was rewarding. In Edinburgh we walked the Royal Mile from the castle to the Palace of Holyrood house. There was a Wanderlust Café and Bistro nearby where we had a family gathering that included Barbara and Patrick, Charlie's daughter Ann, Alexander (Harry's and Oleńka's oldest son), and his wife Caroline.

The next day I drove 350 miles (564 kilometers) from Edinburgh to King's Stanley in a rented car, having adapted to the British system of driving six years earlier. The road passes between the big cities of Leeds, Manchester, Birmingham, and Coventry toward the east and Liverpool toward the west, situated on the Mersey Estuary close to the Irish Sea.

Oleńka and her husband, Harry, made their guest bedroom available for me, and we watched fragments of an opening game of the World Cup in Japan and South Korea between France and Senegal, which Senegal surprisingly won 1:0. Then we went out to eat at the Woolpack Inn restaurant in Stroud. The Scottish and European food suited us well. I also met their daughter, Mariann. Their youngest son, Nicholas, was away on vacation (or holiday in British English) at that time.

I perfunctorily followed the World Cup in South Korea and Japan in June. It was the first World Cup for Poland after a sixteen-year absence; however, the United States was making its fourth straight appearance. Interestingly, both teams were assigned to Group D, and it was the US team that played positively, securing qualification after the first two games with a win over favored Portugal and a draw with South Korea. Poland was eliminated after two losses and no goals scored against South Korea and Portugal. The US team could afford to lose 1:3 to Poland in a meaningless game and later reach the quarterfinal, where it lost in unlucky circumstances to Germany. Brazil defeated Germany 2:0 in the final.

The drive to London and boarding the plane at Gatwick Airport went smoothly, and approximately two hours and forty minutes later I arrived in Lisbon. Amazingly, my family was there at the gate, looking slightly anxious, but content that I had managed to get there in a very efficient manner. (They did too!)

Our trip took us from Lisbon through Fatima, by train to Madrid, Spain, and then in a rented car through the Basque Country to France, including Lourdes and the Loire Valley to Paris, where we would part.

2.

We started with a good look at the magnificent city of Lisbon, mainland Europe's westernmost capital city. It lies in the western Iberian Peninsula on the Atlantic Ocean and the River Tagus. It is one of the oldest cities in the world, established before the eighth century BC, and it is the second oldest European capital city, after Athens. It was part of the Roman Empire and was then ruled by a series of Germanic tribes; later it was captured by the Moors in the eighth century. In 1147, Afonso Henriques, the first king of Portugal, conquered the city, and since then it has been the political, economic, and cultural center of Portugal.

Our hotel was in the center of the city, and the starting point of the tour was the Commerce Plaza (Praca do Comercio), which faces the harbor to the south. Less than a mile to the northeast is St. George's Castle (Castelo de Sao Jorge). The first fortifications were built by Phoenicians; its current structure dates back from the twelfth century.

We briefly saw the Lisbon Cathedral (of Saint Mary Major) and prepared to go to Fatima in a rented Renault car.

Fatima is a village located 78 miles (120 kilometers) northeast of Lisbon. It lies in the municipality of Ourem, district of Santarem. It is known as the site of the apparitions of Mary, Mother of Jesus, to three shepherd children at the Cova da Iria from May 13 to October 13, 1917. The children were Lucia dos Santos and her cousins Francisco and Jacinta Marto. They received visions and prophecies that are known as the Three Secrets of Fatima. The first secret concerned the vision of Hell; the second secret concerned the establishment of worldwide devotion to the Immaculate Heart of Mary and the outbreak of World War II if people did not mend their ways after World War I. There would be "spreading of the errors of Russia" around the world, causing discord, wars, and persecution of the Church. The Third Secret remains a subject of disputes about whether the specific visions of the suffering of the pope were fulfilled in the failed assassination attempt on John Paul II on May 13, 1981, or if they are still unfolding. (In the vision, the pope is killed by a group of soldiers with bullets and arrows; there was one gunman on May 13, and John Paul II survived.) Also, in the Third Secret there is an allusion to a crisis affecting the highest levels of the Church, a worldwide apostasy (falling away from the faith). Our Lady asked for a Consecration of Russia by the pope in union with all the bishops of the world in a separate apparition on June 13, 1929, in Tuy, Spain, where Sister Lucia was stationed at that time, to avert the calamities, wars, and possible annihilation of nations. She also asked that the Third Secret be made public by the year 1960. The Third Secret contained difficult prophecies and visions, which could be averted. However, the pope in 1960 decided not to reveal it as requested by Our Lady. Instead, the preparations for the Second Vatican Council were set afoot.

The Sanctuary of Our Lady of the Rosary in Fatima (Santuario de Nossa Senhora do Rosario de Fatima) is a large building with a vast square in front of it. There is a Chapel of the Apparitions on the left, when facing the church. It contains the area where three children said the Virgin Mary first visited them. There is a statue of Our Lady inside the protective glass, with a crown in which was placed the bullet retrieved from John Paul II's abdomen after the shooting on May 13, 1981.

There is a larger Basilica of the Holy Trinity across from the main sanctuary, designed for large scale pilgrimages and religious services.

This is certainly an important place, religiously and historically. There are monuments commemorating the events of the last century, including the tombs of the visionaries. The story of Fatima still impacts the world today, with its problems and conflicts.

We spent the whole afternoon in Fatima and returned to Lisbon in the evening. The next day we visited the rest of the Alfama neighborhood with its narrow, steep, cobblestone streets and its cafes. We saw the impressive Monument of the Discoveries (Padrao dos Descobrimentos) in Santa Maria de Belem, to the west of Alfama and the city center, on the edge of the Tagus River. There are statues of Prince Henry the Navigator, Vasco da Gama, Ferdinand Magellan (Fernao de Magalhaes), and other famous explorers of the Age of Discovery in the late fifteenth and early sixteenth century.

We had a train ticket to Madrid in the evening and had to return our rental car. There was a miscommunication with the Europcar Car Rental agency, and I thought they would meet us at a certain place and drop us off at the train station. After all of us had sat in the car for an hour, finally something occurred to me, and I gave them another call. They said to bring the car to their office. They still offered us a courtesy car to the Santa Apolonia Railway Station. We boarded the Trenhotel Lusitania train, which took us via Gare de Oriente Station to the Chamartin Station in the center of Madrid in eleven hours. We had comfortable sleeper berths.

The hotel was nearby. It was a nice, clean property of the Melia chain, and it gave us a good vantage point to visit the city.

We rented a car again from Europcar Car Rental. One of the first destinations was the Royal Palace of Madrid (Palacio Real de Madrid), the official residence of the Spanish royal family, although now used only for state ceremonies. With its floor area of about 1.4 million square feet (135,000 square meters), it is the largest functioning palace in Europe.

We saw the famous landmarks of the city, Plaza Major and Puerta del Sol (Gate of the Sun), which serves as the kilometer zero from which all radial roads in Spain are measured. From there we went to the Prado Museum (Museo Nacional del Prado), with the famous works of Francisco Goya, El Greco, Peter Paul Rubens, Titian, and Diego Velasquez. It is certainly one of the most illustrious collections of Spanish and European art.

The next day we drove to Segovia, sixty miles (ninety kilometers) in the northwest direction, a city famous for its historic buildings, including three landmarks: its midtown Roman Aqueduct, the Cathedral, and the medieval castle that served as one of the templates for Walt Disney's Cinderella Castle. The aqueduct was built in the first century AD to channel water from the springs in the mountains eleven miles (seventeen kilometers) away to the city and was in use until 1973. It is present prominently in the city's coat of arms. The cathedral is one of the latest to be built in Europe that follows a Gothic style. The city of Avila is forty miles (sixty-four kilometers) southwest of Segovia. It is the birthplace of St. Teresa of Avila, a Carmelite nun, mystic, and religious reformer who was declared a Doctor of the Church in 1970. Regrettably, we did not reach it.

In Madrid we passed the famous Santiago Bernabeu soccer stadium, home of the winningest European Club in all international competitions, Real Madrid CF, and glanced at it from the outside. Two years later, in August 2004, I would be there again to watch the game between Real Madrid and Polish champions Wisła Kraków in the Champions League qualifying competition. It would regrettably be without my family. Deep fissures in communication had formed by then between us.

3.

We then drove to Donostia-San Sebastian, a resort town on the Bay of Biscay in Spain's mountainous Basque Country. It is 300 miles (480 kilometers) from Madrid, and only twelve miles (twenty kilometers) from the France-Spain border. The capital of the province Bilbao is sixty miles (one hundred kilometers) to the west. Further west are places of importance for Catholics: one is of another reported apparition of Mary in San Sebastian de Garabandal. Another is in the northwest Galicia region, its capital, Santiago de Campostela, with a famous cathedral that is the burial place of St. James the Greater, one of the apostles of Jesus Christ.

The beaches of San Sebastian, Zurriola, La Concha and Ondarreta, offer sunbathing, water, and restaurants with local wines (a lightly sparkling txakoli) that are renowned for their cuisine, including fresh oysters. We stayed at the beachside apartment, only yards from the beach and water and only one kilometer from the city center. The restaurant served superb crepes for breakfast, with fruits and juices.

The walk on the beach was refreshing. We had one day with clouds and intermittent drizzle. The next morning, we drove 120 miles (200 kilometers) to Lourdes in France. Lourdes is straight east of San Sebastian, in the region of Occitania in southern France.

We checked into a hotel close to the Sanctuary of Our Lady of Lourdes, built around a site of the Lourdes apparitions of Mary in February 1858, in the grotto of Massabielle (which means "the ancient rock" in the local Bigorre dialect).

The sanctuary consists of the Basilica of Our Lady of the Immaculate Conception (upper basilica), The Rosary Basilica (lower basilica), and Basilica of St. Pius X (underground basilica).

The sanctuary is a destination for sick and disabled pilgrims, as the Lourdes water, which has flowed from the grotto since the apparitions, is reputed for miraculous healings. An estimated 200 million people have visited the shrine since 1860 (second only to Rome for Catholic pilgrimage sites), and the Church has officially recognized sixty-nine healings as miraculous.

There is a five-domed St. Mary's Ukrainian Catholic Church, whose interior polychrome decorations were executed by artist Jerzy Nowosielski (1923–2011), a relative on my mother's side of the family. We were not aware of it at the time of our visit.

Lourdes has four museums: the Wax Museum, Pyrenean Museum, Museum of the Nativity, and Museum of Small Lourdes. I recall the first one the most; it shows realistic, well executed religious scenes.

On the evening of our first day, there was a prayer service at the basilica, but I'd had an extra glass (or two) of wine with dinner following the promptings of a very hospitable waiter, and my disposition was not proper for the occasion. The strange feeling related to the elevated uric acid level persisted.

Our visit to the grotto during the second and only full day in Lourdes was memorable and moving. Above the main recess is the niche where Our Lady, seen by Bernadette Soubirous, was standing during the apparitions and where her statue now stands. The spring that St. Bernadette discovered can be seen at the rear of the grotto, shielded by a glass cover. Lourdes water is available for pilgrims at water taps located near the grotto along the Massabielle rock. There are two separate places for water distribution, one for drinking and filling bottles, and another to take water as a religious gesture, as Our Lady told St. Bernadette to drink it and wash herself with it. There are also baths of water in which the pilgrims can immerse. We took two small bottles of water with us to Bismarck and used it for ailments. I prayed that it would cure Gosia of her multiple sclerosis but was there a full measure of faith?

We had to leave the next morning and drive north through the regions of Occitaine and Aquitaine to the Center Region, renamed in 2015 as Centre Loire Valley (Centre-Val de Loire). The region is known for its historic châteaux (manor houses) of nobility or gentry. There are over three hundred chateaux in the region, ranging from practical fortified castles from the tenth century to splendid Renaissance residences built in the 1500s. These were built on hilltops such as Chateau d'Amboise or Chateau de Montsoreau, the only one on the riverbed. We stopped at the Chateau de Chambord, the largest in the valley, which is on the most direct way to Paris. The King of France Francis I (1494–1547) oversaw its construction as his hunting lodge. The building blends traditional French medieval forms with classical renaissance structures. The chateau was never intended to be a defensive fortress; consequently, the walls, towers, and partial moat are decorative. The roofline is unique, consisting of eleven kinds of towers and three types of chimneys. It has been compared with the skyline of a town rather than the salient points of a single building. The centerpiece of the chateau is a double-spiral staircase that ascends three floors, the two spirals never meeting.

The chateau is surrounded by a 13,000-acre wooded park and game reserve, enclosed by a nineteen-mile (thirty-one-kilometer) wall.

We stayed overnight at a small hotel near Orleans, thirty miles away in the northeast direction, and were ready in the morning to drive the remaining ninety miles to Paris.

4.

Paris had good signage coming from the south to get to the center of the city where we had our hotel. When I look back at our travels, it surprises me that we could find the addresses well without the elaborate GPS systems as they exist in contemporary cars. (The vehicle I purchased a year later, a 2003 Cadillac Escalade, was the first to have a built-in GPS. I also used a dash cam, purchased at Best Buy, in future vehicles that were not equipped with it.) Paper maps existed before the advent of electronics, and they served well (and still do!).

We checked into Hotel Cecilia, near the Arc de Triomphe (Triumphal Arch), at the western end of the Champs-Elysees at the center of Place

Charles de Gaulle, formerly named Place d'Etolie (Place of the Star), at the juncture formed by its twelve radiating avenues. The location was convenient to reach all the famous landmarks of Paris with ease.

We saw all the usual places of interest including the Notre Dame Cathedral and the nearby Sainte-Chapelle, commissioned by King St. Louis IX in 1238 to house his collection of the relics of Christ's Passion, including the Crown of Thorns.

The cathedral is a masterpiece of French Gothic architecture. It has flying buttresses outside, colorful rose windows, abundant sculptural decoration, three organ pipes, and immense church bells.

In April 2019, the roof caught fire during the renovation, and the building sustained damage. It is stabilized now. It will be restored preserving the "historic, artistic, and architectural interest," and it is hoped that it will be functioning as a religious site again in 2024 in time for the opening of the Summer Olympics in Paris.

We could not miss the Eiffel Tower, one kilometer south from the Arc and the Louvre Museum and three kilometers to the east. There were huge crowds lined up in the courtyard to see the Mona Lisa, Venus de Milo, and other priceless masterpieces. The Louvre Museum is the most visited museum in the world, with 7.7 million people in 2021, even more than the Vatican Museum, which is in second place with 5.1 million.

There remained for us to see the Hotel des Invalides ("house of invalids"), a complex of buildings in the seventh arrondissement of Paris (administrative district, one of twenty), with museums, monuments, a hospital, and a retirement home for war veterans. There is the former Royal Chapel, known as the Dome des Invalides, the tallest church building in Paris at a height of 107 meters. There is a Tomb of Napoleon in an open crypt, beneath the dome.

The Pantheon is nearby, as well as the Saint-Etienne-du-Mont church, which contains the shrine of St. Genevieve, the patron saint of Paris.

Ninety-two people are interred or commemorated in the Pantheon, which is allowed only by a parliamentary act. Among them are politicians, writers, clergymen, and scientists, including Polish-born Maria Skłodowska-Curie, the only person to win the Nobel Prize in two sciences (physics in 1903 and chemistry in 1911) and her husband Pierre Curie, co-winner in 1903; they are the first married couple to receive the Nobel Prize jointly.

Our time in Paris concluded quickly. As with the situation in Lisbon, there was a little difficulty with returning our rental car. It was hard to find the office; I did not speak any French at the time, and, in accordance with the prevailing wisdom, the Parisians are not eager to speak English with the American tourists. I finally found the right place, returned the car, and returned on foot to the hotel. We used a hotel van to get to Charles de Gaulle Airport. We parted ways to go in different directions. My family flew to Warsaw to spend the next two weeks in Poland. I returned to Bismarck. Gosia, her dad, and the children went to Gdynia for a week, our previous destination in 2000.

5.

These were the last days of June and first days of July. I was eager to return to the office, resume seeing patients, and continue the fen-phen echocardiographic screening program. Things looked stable and promising enough.

I almost immediately directed my steps to a Catholic church in Mandan that had Masses in Latin. I was growing uncomfortable about many aspects of the Liturgy in a modern parish. We technically still belonged to the Cathedral of the Holy Spirit Parish, and our children continued their religious education there. Adam and Alek would later receive the Sacrament of Confirmation.

I immediately felt at home at St. Michael's; it was then a mission parish of the Society of St. Pius X (SSPX), and the priest flew into town every other Sunday.

After my family came from Poland, I shared the news with them about St. Michael's Church with Latin Mass, but Gosia, Ania, and Alek weren't interested. Adam was the only one who wanted to become familiar with the church and even played violin at Masses at times. (Adam later became a violinist for the Bismarck Symphony Orchestra and then in the Fargo ensemble while studying at Concordia College in Moorhead, Minnesota.)

As the year 2003 began, the team of Wisła Kraków, with whom I had emotional connections since childhood thanks to Grandfather Lolek, was playing well and had won two League Championships in the past three seasons. By virtue of finishing second in the 2001–2002 season, it qualified for the UEFA Cup, a second-tier competition in Europe, and played extremely well, eliminating Italian team AC Parma and German team Schalke 04 Gelsenkirchen in the fall of 2002. It drew 3:3 in Rome on February 20 against SS Lazio in the first leg (of the round of 16). The second leg of the tie was scheduled for February 27, and I flew to Kraków to meet with Rysiek and watch the game, which we thought would be winnable for Wisła. At that time, the "away goals rule" was still in effect, so a low scoring draw (0:0, 1:1, or 2:2) would promote the Polish team. Of course, any victory would, too.

We bought the tickets at the entrance to the stadium and took our places under the stadium rooftop. It was the grandstand of the stadium, so the viewing of the game would be traditional, as it is usually broadcast on TV.

Something, unfortunately, did not feel right from the beginning. There was a delay in the introduction of both teams, at first ten minutes, then fifteen, then half an hour. Finally, the announcement came that the Italian club was refusing to play the game because "the pitch is frozen, it is too dangerous." It was true that the weather was not necessarily balmy, but it was not the worst to imagine. It was obvious that the Italians were playing the psychological game. The coaches of both teams, Henryk Kasperczak of Wisła and Roberto Mancini of Lazio, were accomplished professionals as players and managers, and the stakes were high. Unfortunately, the game was postponed for a week, and I flew across the Atlantic Ocean twice with not much to show for it. We obtained minor consolation by driving back to Warsaw in Rysiek's car and watching the professional boxing match for the WBA Heavyweight Championship between Roy Jones Jr. and John Ruiz, in which Junior prevailed over "The Quietman" by unanimous decision.

I returned to Bismarck, went back to work, and watched the highlights of the game a week later on March 5. Wisła lost 1:2, despite taking the lead in the fifth minute but then conceding two goals. They hit the post at the end of the game, but it was not to be. The pitch was worked on for a few days, but strangely enough, the Scottish referee twisted his ankle during the game and had to be replaced by the assistant referee. The game, as the miniature of life, is unpredictable.

Lazio was eliminated in the semifinal by the eventual winners, FC Porto of Portugal.

Wisła slowly modernized their stadium, including installation of the heated turf, but they have not repeated their peak form of 2002–2003. They could not reach the group stage of the Champions League, although they were very close on two occasions: in 2005, losing to Panathinaikos of Athens under very controversial circumstances when the English referee favored the Greek team in the last minute of the game; and in 2011, narrowly losing to APOEL of Cyprus. In fact, both times there was a problem with the completion of the last stand of the stadium to meet UEFA (European Football Association) specifications of the Champions League competition. Since 2011 Wisła has slid downwards, and in 2022 it was relegated to the second tier of domestic competition. In 2005 I followed the games while working as a locum in Sault-Ste. Marie, Michigan, and in 2011 while working in Syracuse, New York, for MEPCOM (Military Entrance Processing Command).

6.

In May Rysiek paid a return visit and came to Bismarck. He enjoyed the sights, our house, and my office. We toured our usual local attractions: the capitol with the Natural History Museum, the cathedral, the Missouri River, and the Custer House. We stopped at Caspar's East 40 and Peacock Alley.

After one week in Bismarck, we took a journey in our '02 Chevy Tahoe to New York, from where Rysiek would be departing for Poland. We paused in Minneapolis-St. Paul and Chicago, went to the Willis Tower and Michigan Avenue, viewed the Basilica of St. Hyacinth on West Wolfram Street, and saw the Holy Trinity Church on North Noble Street. We walked up and down Milwaukee Avenue, which was the home of Polish restaurants, delicatessens, and bookstores.

We used the I-80 tollway to drive eastwards past Toledo, Cleveland, and Pittsburgh before turning southward on I-76 toward Washington, DC. The time to change oil arrived along the way, and the service station convinced me that there were "excessive carbon deposits" on the engine that they needed to expunge for an additional $65. They did it by spraying a substance on the engine that produced thick smoke. Business makes the world go around, but one should say "no" to a deal if necessary.

We reached the nation's capital quickly, covering seven hundred miles in eleven hours. We visited all the landmarks carefully and attentively, including Arlington National Cemetery, stopping at the graves of Presidents John F. Kennedy and William H. Taft, Senator Robert F. Kennedy, boxing world heavyweight champion Joe Louis, and other notable graves and landmarks. The United States Marine Corps War Memorial (Iwo Jima Memorial) was nearby. There is obviously a special atmosphere in this place, with the palpable weight of history and human endeavors in earthly lives facing their eternal destiny.

The next day we devoted almost entirely to visiting the National Shrine of the Immaculate Conception, in the northeastern part of the city. It is a large minor Catholic basilica, which was consecrated on September 23, 1920, dedicated to the Immaculate Conception of Our Lady on November 20, 1959. There was recent work done on the central Trinity Dome, creating a mosaic by installing twenty-four tons of Venetian glass (we had an idea of this kind of art after our visit to Murano in Venice in 2000). It was dedicated on December 8, 2017, the Feast of the Immaculate Conception. There is a Great Upper Church, which seats nine thousand people, and the Lower Church (Crypt Church), which seats an additional thousand. Paul VI's "Milan tiara" is in the Crypt Church; he renounced it at the end of the II Vatican Council. An act of hubris may be misconstrued as an act of humility, and it may be a symbolic indication of a pattern in the developments since October 1958, which replaces the teaching, sanctifying, and ruling role of the papacy and the Church with "the primacy of conscience" and replacement of the sacred disciplines of Divine Revelation with purely secular premises, perspectives, and priorities.[2]

After visiting the side chapels and spending some time in prayer, we retired to the cafeteria. I spent extra time inside the basilica's bookstore, which had a tremendous selection of books, albums, calendars, religious articles, and souvenirs. I finally bought a book (after at least two hours of reading it) by Fr. Charles Arminjon (1824–1885), titled *The End of the Present World and the Mysteries of the Future Life*. It is a captivating book, based on a thorough understanding of the Scriptures by the author, who applies a sweeping view to our journey through life. He makes the afterlife palpable and, indeed, less of a mystery for the reader. I still have this book on the shelf after twenty years and four moves.

We drove to Baltimore and Philadelphia the next day. In Baltimore we stopped briefly at the Basilica of the National Shrine of the Assumption of the Blessed Virgin Mary. It was the first Roman Catholic Cathedral built in the United States between 1806 and 1821, designed by Benjamin H. Latrobe and consecrated by Ambrose Marechal, the third Archbishop

2   les femmes-thetruth.blogspot.com. July 6, 2023.

of Baltimore.

The church is built in the neoclassical style, designed in conformity to a Latin cross basilica plan. The plan unites a domed space and a longitudinal axis. Notable interments include John Carroll (1735–1815), the first bishop of the United States; Ambrose Marechal (1764–1828); and James Cardinal Gibbons (1834–1921), the ninth archbishop of Baltimore.

From Baltimore we reached Philadelphia in the evening. The distance between the two historic American cities is only 105 miles, and the drive took just under two hours.

We chose Philadelphia Marriott Downtown as our lodging for two nights. Our first steps were to the Independence National Historical Park and Independence Hall, which has been in the National Register of Historic Places since 1966 and a World Heritage Site since 1979. The Liberty Bell was in the steeple of the Independence Hall (originally Pennsylvania State House) but is now across the street in the Liberty Bell Center. The bell did not ring on July 4, 1776, because the vote for independence was not immediately announced, but it was rung on July 8 to mark the reading of the United States Declaration of Independence. The bell acquired its distinctive crack in the nineteenth century. A widespread story claims it cracked while ringing after the death of Chief Justice John Marshall in 1835.

From there we walked to the Logan Circle (or Logan Square); the Cathedral Basilica of Saints Peter and Paul was just steps away. It is an imposing building, designed by Napoleon LeBrun and built between 1846 and 1864. The interior of the basilica was largely decorated by Constantino Brumidi, a naturalized American of a Greek and Italian extraction, who also decorated the senate corridors in the United States capitol. There is a National Shrine of Saint John Neumann, 2.5 miles to the northeast. The saint was born in Czechia in 1811, came to the United States in 1836, joined the Redemptorist Order, became the fourth bishop of Philadelphia, and was the first male American citizen to be canonized, in 1977.

Philadelphia Museum of Art and its famous steps were just one mile to the west. At that time, the statue of Rocky was still at the top of the seventy-two steps leading to the museum; since 2006 it has been at the bottom in an enclosed area. Philadelphia is known as "The City of Brotherly Love," yet an apt nickname for the home to the city of 1.6 million people could easily be "Fight City." Some of the most beloved, respected, celebrated, and admired fighters in boxing history came from there, such names as Joe Frazier, Jimmy Young, Meldrick Taylor, Bernard Hopkins, and, in earlier times, Tommy Loughran.

We wanted to go to the NBA Eastern Conference Semifinals game between the Philadelphia 76ers and the Detroit Pistons. It was the sixth game, played on May 16 in what was then known as the First Union Spectrum, the name at the time being a commercial acknowledgment of the sponsor of the first modern sports arena in the city, built in 1967 (The Spectrum). We walked toward the arena, which is south of downtown, and were met by a person who said he had two tickets to the game for sale. I forked over $200, and we thought we would have almost VIP seating with unrivalled views. Unfortunately, after arriving at the entrance to the stadium, an official-looking person at the turnstiles told us the tickets were fake. We bought two regular tickets for under $100 and had decent seats.

The game was exciting, and the announcer kept the atmosphere heated to the maximum. The game went into overtime, and the Pistons prevailed 93:89. The Sixers' star Allen Iverson played every minute of the game and scored 38 points; the Pistons had a little more balanced team with Ben Wallace, Chauncey Billups, and Richard Hamilton. Derrick Coleman and Keith van Horn supported Iverson in the Philadelphia frontcourt. Detroit lost to the New Jersey Nets in the Eastern Conference Final. San Antonio was the overall winner that year. I did not follow NBA afterwards, focusing on work and other projects, sports, and hobbies.

The last leg of our trip was to New York City, ninety-five miles away, which required one hour and forty minutes by car. We rented a room at the Holiday Inn in Brooklyn.

This was my sixth or seventh trip to the Big Apple, the first one after the 9/11 terrorist attacks. We directed our steps to the World Trade Center site, which was a painful scar in Lower Manhattan, secured by then and being prepared for reconstruction. We looked at the huge crater, the site of so much destruction and death less than two years earlier. We knew that the repercussions of this event would be felt for years and decades to come.

Rysiek and I visited the Metropolitan Museum of Art, which is about six miles north of the World Trade Center site, and we combined walking and using the subway. It is the eighth largest museum in the world in terms of the annual visits from 3.2 million people. The permanent collection includes works of art from classical antiquity and ancient Egypt, paintings and sculptures from nearly all the European masters, and an extensive collection of American and modern art. The Met maintains extensive holdings of African, Asian, Oceanian, Byzantine, and Islamic art. The museum is also home to collections of musical instruments, costumes and accessories, and antique weapons and armor from around the world. The "Washington Crossing the Delaware" oil-on-canvas painting by Emanuel Leutze is in the American wing. Another version of the painting is in the Minnesota Marine Art Museum in Winona, Minnesota.

There was a painting of Saint Peter as the first pope wearing a papal tiara, otherwise clothed in a tunic worn in the Holy Land in the first century. This was an allegory, since the first proven document of the designation of a tiara as papal head-covering refers to the life of Paschal II (1099–1118) in the *Liber Pontificalis* (a book of papal biographies from St. Peter until the fifteenth century). In the discussion that ensued, I maintained that the scriptural, doctrinal, and historical evidence is irrefutable that Peter was indeed the first pope. Rysiek postulated that this was a retrospective claim made by the Catholic Church in later centuries.

The popes of the first millennium are shown in later paintings as wearing tiaras, such as Pope Constantine (708–715), in whose life the tiara is first mentioned. It was then called a *camelaucum* in the *Liber Pontificalis*. The tiara was a ceremonial, non-liturgical vestment, used during ceremonial processions or while proclaiming solemn acts of authority. The second period of the development of the tiara extends to the pontificate of Boniface VIII (1294–1303), who put forward some of the strongest claims of any pope to temporal and spiritual power, including a document (papal bull-decree) Unam Sanctam, issued on November 18, 1302, which proposes dogmatically the position of the pope as supreme head of the Church and supremacy of spiritual power over temporal. I mentioned the papal tiara on display at the National Shrine of the Immaculate Conception in Washington, DC. There are twenty-three papal tiaras in existence, the oldest one from the pontificate of Gregory XII (1572–1585).

This museum was certainly an enlightening experience. From there we went to Central Park, which is one mile away, and then to St. Patrick's Cathedral, another priceless religious, architectural, and cultural gem. It lies between 50th and 51st streets, Fifth Avenue and Madison Avenue. Archbishop Fulton Sheen, the famous TV preacher who died on December 9, 1979, was buried at St. Patrick's Cathedral initially until his remains were transferred in 2019 to St. Mary's Cathedral in Peoria, Illinois, where he was ordained a priest in 1919.

The Rockefeller Center is next to the cathedral. Heading south we visited Times Square with all the glitzy neon lights and then headed to Lower Manhattan for a farewell supper near the hotel before Rysiek's approaching departure.

7.

My friend took off from the JFK Airport in the morning, and I started driving north on I-87 toward the Canadian border. The distance from New York to Montreal is 370 miles, a six-hour drive. The road became I-15 in the Province of Quebec, and I quickly reached Montreal, the largest city in Quebec and the second largest in Canada after Toronto in the Province of Ontario. It was founded in 1642 as Ville-Marie or "City of Mary." It is named after Mount Royal, the triple-peaked hill around which the early city of Ville-Marie was built. I stayed at the Residence Inn Hotel in downtown Montreal, one mile from the Notre-Dame Cathedral. It is one of the most beautiful churches in the world, a masterpiece of Gothic Revival architecture, built in 1823–1829. The interior of the church is dramatically colorful. The vaults are colored deep blue and are decorated with golden stars, and the rest of the sanctuary is decorated in blues, azures, reds, purples, silver, and gold. The stained-glass windows along the walls of the sanctuary do not depict biblical scenes but rather scenes from the religious history of Montreal.

Saint Joseph's Oratory is six to seven miles in the southwestern direction from the cathedral, but I did not visit it. It is located in the Cote-des-Neiges neighborhood in the geographic center of the Island of Montreal. It was founded in 1904 by Saint Andre Bessette in honor of his patron, Saint Joseph, and finally completed in 1967. It is the highest building in Montreal, rising more than thirty meters above Mount Royal's summit. (This technically violates the height restriction under the municipal building code of Montreal.) As in the Washington, DC basilica, there is the main church (the shrine, which encompasses the nave, apse, and transept) and the crypt church. The Votive Chapel of Saint Joseph is always surrounded by candles. The body of Saint Andre Bessette (Brother Andre) is interred in the vault behind it. When he died on January 6, 1937, at the age of ninety-one, over a million people filed past his coffin. He was beatified in 1982 and canonized in 2010.

A trip to Quebec City was unfortunately not possible (about 160 miles due east). Fairmont Le Chateau Frontenac, a historic hotel in Old Quebec, is one of the first completed grand railway hotels (in 1893), following the buildings in Montreal (1878) and Banff, Alberta (1888). The largest railway hotel is in Toronto, built in 1931; the last one was built in 1958 in Montreal.

Instead, I headed west, back to the United States and back to Bismarck. From Montreal to Windsor is 556 miles (896 kilometers). It is possible to make it in one day, skipping Ottawa, which is further north, and seeing downtown Toronto only from the window of the car while driving on Route 401 in Ontario. The skyline of downtown Toronto is impressive with its 1815 ft CN Tower (referred to the Canadian National Railway company), still the tallest free-standing structure in the Western Hemisphere and currently number ten in the world.

The drive was pleasant, if a bit tedious at the end, and I checked into a Comfort Inn on Dougall Avenue. After a refreshing night and good breakfast, I crossed the border via Detroit-Windsor Tunnel and found myself on the "home turf." Detroit is a historic city, and I would have three more occasions to visit it, in 2009, 2011, and 2017, each time the leitmotif being the Solanus Casey Center on Mount Elliott Street. There is a spiritual connection between Solanus Casey, Andre Bessette, and Pio of Pietrelcina in Italy. Each one was a doorkeeper, a healer, and a saint (although Blessed Solanus is still awaiting official canonization by the Church; I was at Ford Field in October 2017 for his beatification ceremony).

I divided the remaining distance of 1,115 miles to Bismarck into two parts, resting in Tomah, Wisconsin, for the night and finally being able to greet my family again the next afternoon.

8.

I applied myself to work and the usual routine and saw patients for two months until cousin Bożena (daughter of my father's brother Lesław, who visited my parents in 1996 and joined them on a trip from Missouri to Nebraska, the Dakotas, Montana, Wyoming, and Colorado) and her daughter, Katarzyna (Kasia), came to Bismarck to visit us in July. We toured our usual places of interest—restaurants, museums, the mall—and then headed west to Medora and the Badlands.

This time the experience of the pitchfork fondue and the Musical in the Burning Hills Amphitheater was particularly memorable. I joined in the singing of the National Anthem and thought that Bożena and Kasia were also moved. (Kasia later married an American gentleman, Paul, so maybe this trip planted the fondness for America in her heart.) We reached the accessible points of the Theodore Roosevelt National Park and did horseback riding at the Maah Daah Hey Trail. We visited the central, historic part of town, which had been developed further since that time. Medora takes its name from the wife of Marquis de Mores (de Vallombrosa), a frontier rancher in the Badlands of Dakota Territory in the 1880s. He was devoted to many adventurous pursuits in his life in his native France, Vietnam, Algeria, and Tunisia, where he was finally ambushed and assassinated by the Touaregs (an ethnic group of northern and western Sahara) around Kebili. In 1882 he married Medora von Hoffman, an American heiress, daughter of a wealthy New York banker, Louis von Hoffman, and his wife Athenais. They had three children, opened a stagecoach business, and tried to revolutionize the ranching industry by shipping refrigerated meat to Chicago by railroad, but the Chicago Stock Yard opposed his effort. His range-fed beef turned out to be less popular with consumers than corn-fattened beef in the stockyards of Chicago. His business closed.

He felt resentment and, turning to politics, organized a movement that mixed socialism with antisemitism. After selling their meatpacking business and other assets in the Badlands in 1886, and later, after her husband's death in 1896 during his final wild scheme to unite Muslims in a "holy war" against the British and the Jews, Medora settled in France to live in Paris and Cannes. She died in 1921 after sustaining a wound in her leg while tending to the wounded soldiers during World War I.

The Chateau de Mores built in 1883 still stands in Medora, as does the Von Hoffman House, which was built in 1884.

Mount Rushmore was impressive as always; we spent extra time at The Lincoln Borglum Visitor Center and watched *The Shrine*, a short film that introduces the memorial, which is shown every twenty minutes. The Mount Rushmore Bookstore offered postcards, booklets, and souvenirs. The helicopter tours over Mount Rushmore were a thrilling experience for my Polish family and for myself. A fifteen-minute ride cost forty-nine dollars per person. We had a good look at the monument from all sides and the surrounding Black Hills. I overcame the mild unease of flying in a small aircraft; Bożena and Kasia did not show any anxiety at all, quite the contrary.

We travelled to Minneapolis-St. Paul, which never lose their appeal for me. We attended Sunday Mass at St. Peter's Catholic Church. I felt the difference between the vernacular liturgy and the Latin liturgy, but Bożena was content to fulfill Sunday obligation.

This time we returned to Bismarck in the Tahoe. Bożena and Kasia would fly back to Poland in the next two days. I went back to work. I was grateful to maintain invasive cardiology privileges, which brought extra money. In September I traded the Tahoe for a metallic gold 2003 Cadillac Escalade, which had an eight-inch GPS screen.

The Escalade had a soft ride and powerful, 345 hp V8 engine. We used it once or twice on a trip to Twin Cities, and in 2005 I would use it to get to the Michigan Upper Peninsula for my contract work.

Around the same time, I downsized the Ford Heavy Duty truck, going from the F-350 into a gray F-250, still with the same 6.7 L V8 diesel engine.

In the fall we saw the opportunity to buy a Marriott vacation package to fly to Hawaii for Christmas. I arranged the entire trip with their vacation division and booked a five-night stay at Ko Olina Hawaii Marriott for the entire family at a bargain price. We left Bismarck on Monday, December 22, and changed planes in Denver and in Los Angeles at LAX. There is a four-hour time difference between Bismarck and Honolulu; leaving Bismarck at 9 a.m. got us to Honolulu at 7 p.m. We rented a car at the airport.

The hotel was enchanting, with a pleasant restaurant. There was a Fia Fia Polynesian Dinner Show on Tuesday evening featuring drums, comedy, fire knife dancing, and delicious Hawaiian food. The surroundings of the hotel were likewise unrivalled with a great swimming pool and a cove jutting into the cozy beach with the warm, clean sand. Swimming and snorkeling were refreshing to the deepest fibers of the body.

After the first day spent on the beach, we went to the USS Arizona Memorial at Pearl Harbor, which marks the resting place of 1,102 of the 1,177 sailors and Marines killed on USS Arizona during the attack on Pearl Harbor on December 7, 1941, and commemorates the events of that day.

The memorial is accessible only by boat. It straddles the sunken hull of the battleship without touching it. USS Missouri is not far from USS Arizona in Pearl Harbor, placed perpendicularly to the memorial and facing it with its bow. Upon the deck of the USS Missouri, the Japanese surrendered to General Douglas McArthur and Admiral Chester Nimitz, ending World War II in the Pacific. This arrangement is symbolic of the beginning and end of the United States' participation in the war. We then visited the US Army Museum in Hawaii. In the evening we had a "traditional" Polish-style Christmas Eve supper at our hotel room, with a soup resembling borscht, cabbage, fish (Hawaiian cuisine can offer the largest variety in the world) and sweet dessert with hot tea.

On Christmas Day, which fell on Thursday, we went to the Holy Family Catholic Church for Christmas Mass. After experience with

Latin Mass, modern liturgy seemed to be lacking solemnity and gravitas. (I learned later that Latin Mass and the entire ministry of SSPX had been making their first inroads in Hawaii since the 1990s, and is present on a regular basis now, if only once a month.)

We had Christmas dinner at the hotel, and the remainder of the day we devoted to visiting Kapolei (a planned community west of Honolulu) and Waikiki Beach. We took a brief trip around the whole island of Oahu trying to get to the most picturesque places with the best views of the ocean.

We planned our return to Bismarck on Friday, December 26. The flight from Honolulu was in the afternoon, and we landed at LAX at a late hour. I earlier asked my family to let me spend the weekend in Park City, Utah, to experience new slopes. I landed in Salt Lake City on Saturday morning; family would arrive in Bismarck early in the afternoon. It was thirty-six miles from Salt Lake City Airport to my lodging in Park City. The room at Park City Peaks Hotel was modest but comfortable.

The slopes and the snow lived up to my expectations and the information in the media, the Utah tourist industry, and various publications about skiing. Because of the high altitude and low humidity in the region, a combination of climate conditions over the Wasatch Mountains into the Cottonwood Canyons, and the "right" frequency and amount of snowfall, Utah snow crystals tend to be thick and symmetrical and float slowly to the surface, accumulating as fluffy "powder." Salt Lake City had been the site of the Winter Olympics two years earlier, and the Olympic logos were still visible in town.

The variety of runs was excellent, and I did not stay away from the black runs. The Deer Valley Resort is only five minutes away from Park City, and it adds to the variety of the terrain with both long and relatively sedate runs, but also steep chutes for the experts. I chose the blue runs most often, sometimes venturing in the black run territory if I thought that I was properly prepared.

I marked Sunday by going over the prayers and Mass readings for the day before noon.

In the afternoon I found a slope with racing gates set up for a competitive challenge. I skied toward the start area and registered myself for a run. There were ten to twelve gates over a 150- to 175-meter length of a course, and a twenty to thirty-meter vertical drop. My time was within the limit for a bronze medal (a lapel pin) awarded in this Deer® Valley Medalist Challenge. A time of 9.9 seconds or less would have won the gold, 10–11.9 seconds the silver, and 12–13.9 seconds the bronze. I have the pin with me, never forgetting about it after twenty years have passed.

Monday was the last day of skiing, and on Tuesday, December 30, I returned the rented equipment, drove to the airport, and headed back to Bismarck.

9.

As the year 2004 started, the work kept flowing for the time being. I saw enough patients to "keep the doors open," but there were concerns about balancing the books. No additional echocardiography program was appearing on the horizon, and I did not see the possibility to grow the clinic or hire a partner. I shared the call schedule with the colleagues I'd worked with between 1994 and 2001.

In March I drove alone in a gray Ford F-250 to Jackson Hole. Skiing was still fun in my forty-fifth year of life, long drives were nearly so, and the trip had three days of the former (Thursday, Friday, Saturday) and two days of the latter (Wednesday and Sunday). On Sunday I had a moment of reflection before driving and also listened to educational tapes on medical topics and religious conferences by Bishop Fulton Sheen and Father John Hardon, S.J. on an old-style cassette player in the truck.

On my way back to Bismarck, I helped pull a truck with three passengers from the deep snow on the roadside. The engine power, high ground clearance, and towing capacity of the vehicle were sufficient for the intended tasks.

Soon thereafter, Adam and I went to the theater to see Mel Gibson's film, *The Passion of the Christ*, which created a strong impression on us. I return to watching the DVD every few years around Easter. Adam was interested in seeing this film without any encouragement on my part but needed my presence since he was thirteen at the time.

Ania graduated from Century High School in May, and we collectively felt that continuing education in a college in the Twin Cities would be a promising and desired change for her. I had a sense that we would not be able to live in Bismarck for many more years. Ania needed to broaden her experience. The atmosphere at home was sometimes tense. Gosia and I frequently did not see eye to eye; we could not present a unified front for our children and influence their upbringing. Adam and Alek were not quite on their own yet. In the summer we spent almost every available weekend at Lake Sakakawea, enjoying the Sundancer 300, soaking up the sun, and swimming around the boat. Usually, Adam and Alek joined me. In the evening we watched the old tapes on the Sundancer's built-in TV/VCR of *Saturday Night Live*, mostly from 1990s. The sketches with motivational speaker Matt Foley and the Japanese Game Show were funny, bordering on the absurd.

We bought a dark blue 2004 Chevy Aveo, since Adam was nearing the driving age, first with the permit and then quickly graduating to independent use of the vehicle. Gosia found the small car handy for grocery shopping and other errands.

In August I decided to take a momentous trip to Spain and Israel. The communication between Gosia and I was dwindling. I tried to always "wait things out," hoping that one sunny morning a miracle would happen, and we would be functioning again as a couple, united in our common goal of working, raising a family, and being cordial in mutual relations. In the meantime, I was biding my time. I flew from

Bismarck via Minneapolis-St. Paul and Amsterdam to Madrid on Tuesday the 24th. The next day, the second leg of the third round of the Champions League (the last qualifying round before the Champions League proper, the group stage) was taking place. I checked in at the Holiday Inn and went to the famous Estadio Santiago Bernabeu, the site of many triumphs of the Royal Club, including 29 La Liga titles, 9 European Champions Cups (until that time), and many others. Wisła was a ten-time Polish champion until that time and reached the quarterfinal of the Champions Cup in the season 1978/1979. Since that time, Real has added seven more league titles and six European Cups; Wisła added four more league titles but also two agonizing, unlucky defeats in the Champions League final qualifying round in 2005 and 2011.

Wisła did not have a realistic chance of progressing by overturning a two-goal deficit from Kraków a week earlier. They acquitted themselves well in this game, losing 1:3 but scoring the consolation goal. The tickets were not expensive; everything was done in a regular fashion (no scalping), and I had a seat with the group of fans from Poland.

The next day I flew to Tel-Aviv with El Al Airlines. It is a four-and-a-half-hour flight over the Mediterranean Sea. A pleasant gentleman next to me, across the aisle, took his time to introduce me to basic words and phrases in Hebrew. The proceedings at the Ben Gurion Airport went smoothly, but the interview was very thorough, and I was asked repeatedly for the purpose of my visit to Israel, the Holy Land. I answered simply that the reason was to visit the religious sites associated with the life and ministry of Jesus Christ two thousand years ago.

I checked in to the King David Hotel, a member of The Leading Hotels of the World, built with locally quarried pink limestone and overlooking the Old City and Mount Zion.

I had a desire and a plan to visit as many of the important places as possible, having only three days to accomplish it; the Church of the Holy Sepulchre was the first on the list. I easily secured the services of a local guide who spoke good English and was well informed. The church has a site where Jesus was crucified, known as Calvary, and the tomb where he was buried and then resurrected. There is a large slab of stone called The Stone of Unction inside the church, on which the body of Jesus was laid and prepared for burial. It has a sweet aroma, a floral smell around it. The church was built in AD 335 and was demolished in 1009 by a Fatimid (Shia Islam) caliph, Abu Ali Mansur (al-Hakim bi-Amr), as part of a more general campaign against Christian places of worship in Palestine and Egypt.

The Tomb of the Lord is hewn from a natural rock tomb. The present space (rebuilt in 1048, as the previous cave was destroyed in 1009) is called the Holy Sepulchre. This space, arranged as an aedicule (a shrine in the form of a niche), symbolizes the cave in which the Body of Christ was buried. The Via Dolorosa (Sorrowful Way) or Via Crucis (Way of the Cross) starts from the Fortress Antonia and ends at the Holy Sepulchre. It is 600 meters (2,000 feet) long. We reached Mount Zion next and visited Dormition Abbey (a place where Mary ended her earthly life), King David's Tomb, and the Cenacle (The Upper Room, The Room of the Last Supper). I was incredulous in the places that are the foundational stones of Christianity, which make a tourist appreciate the artistry of the monuments and a believer see the places of the events described in the Gospels. That day we visited the Western Wall (known in the West as the Wailing Wall), which is a portion of the larger retaining limestone wall of the hill known to Jews and Christians as the Temple Mount.

The next day we ventured outside of Jerusalem in the afternoon and my guide "farmed me out" to his colleague who took me to Bethlehem. We reached the Church of the Nativity with the grotto, which marks the birthplace of Jesus. There is a silver star marking this place. My guide suggested that I sit with my back toward the star to have a picture taken. I thought it would be entirely improper and I knelt toward the star, turning my head slightly to the camera. The entrance door to the Basilica of the Nativity is less than five feet tall. To pass through this door, the pilgrims and the visitors are forced to bow down as they enter the church. This has theological significance. We must humble ourselves to approach God. The guide said that the liturgy of the Nativity of Jesus can be celebrated in the basilica every day, all year-round.

The souvenirs at the visited places, displayed in kiosks and stands, were precious, and I bought several crucifixes, rosaries, oils, and small bas-relief of the Nativity scene.

The last full day in the Holy Land (it was a Sunday), I was on my own in the rental car and drove to Nazareth, ninety miles north of Jerusalem via Yitzhak Rabin Highway (Route 6), along the border of the West Bank. I veered briefly into the West Bank territory, partly by mistake and partly by curiosity, but turned around quickly at the first roundabout, less than quarter of a mile into it. I visited Basilica of the Annunciation, which was completed and consecrated in 1969. It was established over the site of the house of the Virgin Mary. Earlier Byzantine, Crusader, and the Israeli-period churches existed at or near this place.

Sixteen miles (twenty-five kilometers) to the southwest from Nazareth toward Tel (Mount) Megiddo is the site of the eschatological (related to last things) significance, where the last battle between good and evil (Christ vs. Anti-Christ) will take place at the end of the world (Armageddon). The view of the Jezreel (as it is known in the Old Testament times) Valley, or the Esdraelon (Greek modification of Jezreel) Valley of the vast plain is magnificent. It is reported that when Napoleon Bonaparte first viewed it, he commented that "all the armies in the world could maneuver their forces on this vast plain. [. . .] There is no place in the world more suited for war than this." The plain separates the Galilean hills in the north from Mount Carmel and Mount Gilboa to the south. The feeling of being there cannot be described or compared to anything else. It felt as if one was stepping outside the bounds of time and earthly space.

From Megiddo I drove to Tel-Aviv/Yafo, fifty-five miles further southwest. It is a modern city, established in the early twentieth century, with a population of 468,000 people. I did not have enough time to see the whole city, but in the three or four hours afforded I saw the Promenade (Tayelet), which runs along the seashore, and had dinner at a charming, Mediterranean-style café/restaurant close to the beach and the sea. The fish/seafood entrée was excellent, as was my glass of red wine. The atmosphere of the restaurant was not unlike the one I could experience in Greece, Italy, Spain, or elsewhere in this part of the world. Since there was no possibility of assisting at Mass that day, I reflected quietly on the trip that was just being completed and thanked God for the great experience.

There remained a drive back to Jerusalem to the airport. I already checked out of the hotel, and since the flight back to the US was early in the morning, I had to divide the night between the car, the roadside gas station, and the airport itself. For a while I felt lost in the desert-like landscape without any buildings or other signs of life and started having doubts about which direction I was going. The car did not have GPS. There were signs pointing to a nuclear missile base, and I felt a little uneasy for a moment. Fortunately, the situation was resolved in a brief time; road signs appeared which pointed in the direction of more familiar places, and I finally made it to the airport, returned the car, and boarded the plane to Amsterdam and from there to Bismarck.

10.

Since around 2000, and continuing through 2004, I was driving (occasionally flying) to more conservative, traditionally minded churches in the Twin Cities, usually once every three months. I liked the atmosphere of the church of Saint Agnes on Thomas Avenue, as well as Saint Augustine and Holy Trinity Churches in South St. Paul. At St. Agnes I once met a devout, dignified parishioner, Ms. Genevieve (Genny) Mamai. She came from Kenya, and I felt comfortable sharing in the worship with her and other parishioners in St. Paul from time to time. We did not socialize but were aware of each other. I stopped going to St. Paul at the end of 2006, and there was a complete break in our contacts until the spring of 2012 when we renewed our acquaintance and saw each other on two or three occasions, joined by other friends, either inside the church or at a restaurant or at another friend's house.

I had to sell the boat at the end of the 2004 summer season because of the costs of maintenance and storage. Toys, even the big ones, age quickly, and our needs and wants change, too.

At the end of the year, I needed to supplement my office work with hospital work and decided to function as a locum tenens cardiologist at War Memorial Hospital in Sault Ste. Marie, Michigan. This region of Michigan is called the Upper Peninsula (UP). I signed with Weatherby Locums and Staff Care. The hospital in Bismarck did not renew my invasive procedure privileges; I was ready to work predominantly in an outpatient setting but also see hospital patients.

My plan was for the first two weeks of the month to be out of Bismarck and then condense my office patients into the remaining two weeks. It was a plan that seemed to have caught traction at first. We celebrated the New Years and Alek's thirteenth birthday on Sunday, January 2, 2005; and on Monday morning I left Bismarck in the Escalade, stopping in Duluth, Minnesota, for an overnight rest in a Holiday Inn downtown, reaching Sault Ste. Marie Tuesday evening. I was reimbursed for mileage by the staffing company and provided a hotel room in Sault Ste. Marie. If I chose to drive to work (long commute), the hotel in Duluth, roughly the halfway point, remained my responsibility. The entire distance measured 850 miles, fourteen hours by car. Flying was a bit faster but no less tedious. It took one day, required changing planes in Minneapolis-St. Paul and landing in Traverse City, and driving three hours in a rental car. Usually, I stayed at the Best Western Inn in Sault Ste. Marie.

Sault Ste. Marie is a picturesque city located along the St. Mary's River, which flows from Lake Superior to Lake Huron and forms part of the United States-Canada border. It is the county seat of Chippewa County, the second most populated city in the UP, behind Marquette.

I found the War Memorial Hospital and Clinic easily. The hospital and the clinic staff proved very welcoming. I had a good feeling about the place and felt that everybody wanted to help patients in a compassionate and straightforward fashion. When the situation was too complicated, we requested transfer, usually to UP Health System in Marquette. There was never a problem communicating with doctors in Marquette, and they always gave their best.

I saw patients in the clinic and oversaw exercise stress tests and echocardiograms. There was a second Locum Tenens cardiologist, Dr. Carl Wynter, who came on board shortly after my arrival. He was very methodical with his clinical assessments and echocardiographic reports; it was clear that this area was his specialty. He went on to obtain a subspecialty board certification in echocardiography and nuclear medicine. His involvement with the hospital was more extensive than mine since I returned to Bismarck every two weeks, and he only took a break every four to six weeks.

There was a UP School of Sonography associated with the clinic, operated and run by a friendly and energetic certified sonographer and educator, Mr. Christopher Smith. He had five students that year with him; all of them happened to be women. They were making quick progress in their independent echo skills and were unpretentious and kindhearted to their patients and coworkers.

The hospital administrator was a well-meaning, gentle leader. Mr. Henry Oklat was of Polish extraction, generous in his relating to all physicians, including Dr. Carl and me. That is not to say that he was not demanding and exacting in his duties. Carl and I visited him and his elderly mother at their beautiful house by St. Mary's River with a view of Soo Locks, an intricate construction enabling water transport from Lake Superior to the other Great Lakes.

During the two-week work period in Sault, there was at least one

Sunday off call. I directed my steps to the Holy Name of Mary Proto-Cathedral, established in the then Diocese of Sault Ste. Marie by Pope Pius IX in 1857, transferred to Marquette in 1937. The current building dates from 1881 and serves as a parish church, but it remains a historic, titular episcopal see. (the auxiliary bishop of Chicago holds the title of a titular bishop; the Diocese of Marquette is part of the Ecclesiastical Province of Detroit). Started by Jesuits in 1668 as a parish mission, it is the oldest parish in Michigan and the third oldest in the US after Saint Augustine, Florida, and Santa Fe, New Mexico. Its first bishop was Slovenian-born Venerable Irenaeus Frederic Baraga.

I attended Mass several times but felt internal discomfort at the practices that blurred the distinction between the clergy and laity (women) in terms of the appointed ministries and functions during Mass. It is a widespread practice nowadays, included in just about every aspect of liturgy. In my mind it is an abuse that bulldozes the Catholic character of the liturgy, but unfortunately, one that continues apace, including appointing women to the roles of celebrants, readers, distributors, and others. I stopped going there and made a firm resolution to follow Latin Mass, although it took seventeen more years, until 2022, to stray to the Novus Ordo Mass for the irrevocably last time.

On April 2, John Paul II died, and millions of people went to Rome to pay respects and attend a funeral. Cardinal Joseph Ratzinger, dean of the College of Cardinals, presided at the funeral Mass, which we watched on TV at home in Bismarck. Gosia was moved. Our children were with us, at least for parts of the ceremony. I knew that the battle for the Church would continue; my heart was with SSPX and Tradition, even though I could not attend the Latin Mass regularly. I used booklets and missals to be familiar with prayers and increase my knowledge about Church history, prominent figures of prelates and saints, Doctors of the Church, councils, dogmatic pronouncements, and contemporary developments.

Adam received the Sacrament of Confirmation on April 15, taking the confirmand's name of Pius.

I watched the election of Cardinal Ratzinger as Benedict XVI on April 19 in Sault Ste. Marie. It was during the day, during working hours in the US, and the entire cardiology clinic and echo team gathered in the conference room. I had brief hopes for restoration of liturgical discipline, including Communion on the tongue and general rapprochement with the traditionalist groups. Benedict issued a Motu Proprio, "Summorum Pontificum," liberating Latin Mass in July 2007, but continued ecumenical programs of his predecessors. The day of Benedict's election was an occasion to recall "The Prophecy of the Popes" by St. Malachi, a twelfth-century Irish archbishop. It is a series of 112 short, cryptic phrases that purport to predict the Catholic popes until the last Judgment. All the descriptions of the papal claimants are strongly reflected in the important facets of their lives. One of the persons in attendance noted the description of Benedict as Gloria Olivae (Glory of the Olive) being exactly fulfilled in him, as Benedict had connections with the Olivetans, a branch of the Benedictine Order.

We bought a yellow 2001 Volkswagen New Beetle for Ania in May, after her first year of studies at the University of Minnesota in St. Paul, trading the Cavalier for it. (Ania would later obtain a BA degree in psychology in 2007 and an MA in counseling psychology at the University of St. Thomas in 2011.)

We also downsized from a Ford F-250 to a 2005 Ford F-150 STX extended cab, which would serve me, and from the Escalade to a 2005 Ford Taurus, which would serve Gosia around town.

The rest of the summer and fall went by quickly. I made five more trips to Sault Ste. Marie, but in October the situation changed, and the hospital was keen on hiring full-time cardiologists. Carl and I could not commit to this solution; he decided to continue work in Elkhart, Indiana, and I signed another Locum contract with the Hillsdale Community Health Center & Hospital in south central lower Michigan, near the border with Indiana and Ohio. I worked on a two-week on, two-week off basis, with a break in January and February 2007 due to difficult personal and family goings-on at that time.

During the time of my transition from Sault Ste. Marie to Hillsdale, I enrolled in the University of Mary in Bismarck and took a semester of management theory, organizational communications, and ethics for professionals toward a master of management degree. The classes started in November 2005 and ended in May 2006. I earned nine credits with a GPA of 4.0 with the idea of adding the administrative/business dimension to future work.

In late November, just before Thanksgiving, I decided to fly to Seattle and then drive to Vancouver and Whistler Blackcomb to ski in the Canadian Rockies. My parents came to Bismarck for Thanksgiving, but as a portent of the things to come, I decided to be by myself at that time. There were communication problems between us, and I did not think that bringing them up and discussing them over the holidays would resolve the situation. On the other hand, evasion was not the best approach, either.

The beauty of the Pacific Northwest is still firmly etched in my memory. Seattle is the seat of King County, Washington. I visited the two best known landmarks, the Space Needle, built for the 1962 World's Fair, and Pike Place Market, one of the oldest continuously operated public farmers' markets in the United States. It overlooks the Elliott Bay waterfront on Puget Sound; it is a vibrant place of business for small farmers, crafts, and merchants.

The views from the observation deck were breathtaking, including the downtown Seattle skyline, the Olympic and Cascade Mountains, Mount Rainier, Mount Baker, Elliott Bay, and various islands of Puget Sound.

The 142-mile trip to Vancouver took just over three hours, including the border crossing. Vancouver is as beautiful as Seattle, with an extra Old World charm. It is built on the Burrard Peninsula, surrounded by the majestic mountains and sparkling water of the Burrard Inlet to the north. I looked from afar at Canada Place, Science World, and Vancouver

Art Gallery, and visited Gastown, which is the original settlement that became the core of the city on the south side of the Burrard Inlet. There is an antique-styled steam clock in Gastown, which is the recent work of a Canadian horologist Raymond Saunders. Vancouver Island is further to the west with Victoria, the capital of British Columbia, on its south side.

The seventy-five-mile (120-kilometer) trip to Whistler is incredibly scenic with the town of Squamish along the way, a paradise for all kinds of outdoor activities year-round. I stayed three nights at the Whistler Village Inn and Suites, including the Thanksgiving holiday, and experienced superb skiing for two days, even in the beginning of the season. The snow was wet; one had to take the chairlift from mid mountain to get to the base because there was no packed snow there yet. The terrain was majestic, and the restaurant offered everything that was needed after a good day's workout. I wished I could have stayed longer at the mountain, but time and money factors intervened. I returned to Bismarck on Saturday, November 26th.

Trips to Hillsdale started in December 2005. The trip consisted of a flight to Detroit and renting a car to Hillsdale, a hundred miles away.

Hillsdale Hospital is nestled in a scenic county of some 46,000 residents, with much natural beauty, named for its rolling terrain. Its early settlers came from the northern coastal colonies; "Yankees" descended from the English Puritans who emigrated from the Old World in the 1600s. There was a wave of such settlers in the early 1800s after the completion of the Erie Canal and after the conclusion of the Black Hawk War in 1832. They brought with them a passion for education, establishing many schools. Hillsdale College was founded in 1844. It is a private conservative Christian liberal arts college, which I briefly visited one day. It is 1.5 miles north of the hospital, and I am glad to be still receiving a copy of their free monthly digest, *Imprimis*, dedicated to educating citizens and promoting civil and religious liberty. Its Latin name means both "in the first place" and the second person singular of the verb "to print."

The experience in Hillsdale turned out to be very rewarding. I focused increasingly on general cardiology and set aside diagnostic and therapeutic procedures (echocardiography, stress tests, vascular studies, nuclear medicine, and catheterization), spending more time listening to the patients' personal stories, which in many instances suggested emotional and psychological links to their cardiac symptoms. This approach is helpful in addressing problems in many instances.

I flew to Hillsdale every month but started planning for the next phase of my life. I set the date in my mind for concluding office work by June 2007 and moving back to hospital work in a yet undefined capacity, having an administrative role in mind. Alek received the Sacrament of Confirmation on April 18, 2006, taking the confirmand's name of Leo. In May we adopted a yellow Labrador mix and named him Sam. Gosia and Alek were the initiators of this idea. Sam was a friendly, gentle, wonderful walking companion. Unfortunately, he developed cancer of the lymphatic system in early 2011, and we lost him before Gosia and Alek left for the Twin Cities in June of that year.

The FIFA World Cup in Germany took place from June 9 to July 9. Poland and the United States participated but did not advance from their respective groups. Italy won the final over France on penalty kicks. Germany was third, Portugal fourth.

In the summer and fall of 2006 we changed cars again. I went from a 2005 F-150 STX to 2006 F-150 XLT extended cab, and we traded the '01 New Beetle for a silver 2006 Hyundai Elantra. Ania and her fiancé, Sean, whom she'd met in 2005, purchased a dark brown 2003 Ford Ranger and used it mostly in the Twin Cities and on an occasional visit to Bismarck. (Ania introduced me to Sean in October at an Applebee's restaurant in Roseville. He made a good impression on me as a calm and caring person.) We also purchased a silver 2006 Hyundai Tiburon for Alek, which created a bit of discord with Adam, who did not care about cars that much but felt that he was left out in all these considerations.

He was driving a Chevrolet Aveo at the time. Later we decided to pay much less attention to cars.

11.

In December 2006 I saw the movie *Rocky Balboa* with a group of friends, and we enjoyed it. It was a more fitting conclusion to the Rocky series than *Rocky V* was in 1990. I had seen the original *Rocky* in Bytom in 1976, *Rocky II* in 1979, *Rocky III* in 1982 in Lublin, and *Rocky IV*, which was released in November 1985, in Columbia, Missouri, toward the end of medical school. I am a fan of the series, both as a sports fan in general and because I like the story of an athlete who "disciplines his body and brings it to subjection" (1 Corinthians 9:27), fights many tough opponents, and wins the world heavyweight championship twice. The grueling scenes of training and the fights are well choreographed. I thought that the fight scenes became less scripted as the series went on, with some real punches being thrown between former world-class professional boxer Antonio Tarver (playing an undefeated but "unpopular" boxing champion, Mason "The Line" Dixon) and Sylvester Stallone in the last movie.

Christmas and the New Year holidays were solemn and warm by the fireside at home, but there were signs of trouble brewing. There was poor communication between me on one side and Gosia and Alek on the other. Adam was doing well, trying his best to see both sides of a problem, but the whole situation was taking a toll on him, too. I flew to the Cities to attend Sunday Mass at St. Agnes Church for the last time in mid-January.

I made plans to return to the hospital. The CEO, who had been in this position since 2002, was preparing to move on. I let it be known that I wanted to return to the hospital but did not state my desires openly and did not engage in discussions to build the case for an administrative position. A senior cardiologist was also leaving Bismarck, and major changes were afoot in the hospital. It remained unclear what position I would be returning to at the hospital, if at all.

On the evening of January 22, 2007, I found myself deeply at odds with my family and practically every corner in Bismarck. I think all the groups, teams, and agencies must have thought I was more powerful and important than I really was and treated me without judgement and with clouded reasoning, reaching premature conclusions. The family was united on the opposite side, and I had to simply cut my losses and realize that a new chapter of an uphill battle in my life, first for survival and then for restoration, had begun. Alek had a tough time handling the stress, and I felt disheartened that I could not reach out to him.

I worked very little, if at all, for the rest of January, and in February I completed the administrative work related to closing the office and selling or giving away the equipment. I did not see new patients. I saw my closest patients for a final follow-up, shared the news of leaving Bismarck, and recommended new physicians.

I went to Hillsdale for the last three times in March, April, and May and concluded my service there with gratitude. In May 2007 I sold my treadmill in the Bismarck office to a company in Minnetonka, Minnesota, with the major help of Chris Smith, who connected us and assisted in the negotiating process. The good ties with the UP School of Sonography lasted beyond the time of our initial work in 2005. I concluded work in the Bismarck office in early June 2007 and received an offer for contract work at Fargo Veterans Administration (VA) Hospital to start later in the month.

We sold the F-150 XLT and traded the Taurus for a black 2007 Ford Edge SE. It was a front-wheel drive vehicle, and the traction on the snow and ice was imperfect in the winter. We also sold the Tiburon. The vehicle to guide me to Fargo was the Elantra.

The Fargo VA was not my preferred destination but offered some hope. I wanted to stay close to my family and rebuild the relationships and psychological bonds. I returned home almost every weekend, but, unfortunately, we were not healing or making progress as a family.

In September I traveled to Michigan again to renew ties with Chris and his students. We met in Gaylord, which is in the Northern Lower Peninsula, close to Chris' home. There were minor changes in the school roster, but the students showed the same sincerity and willingness to learn as before. I gave a talk about cardiomyopathies and the role of echocardiography in their diagnosis. (The main types of cardiomyopathy are hypertrophic, dilated, and restrictive, using medical terminology.) Later that evening, after everybody had already left, I saw the highlights of the EURO 2008 qualification game in which Poland bravely drew with Portugal 2:2, equalizing in the very last minute of the game thanks to a skillful (and a bit lucky) shot by Jacek Krzynówek. This ensured the first ever qualification for the European Championship title after twelve failed tries, including the 1976 edition when the team had the quality but lost in October 1975 to the Netherlands 0:3 in an inept game, when even 0:1 would have been enough to advance (because of the overall goal difference). This time both Poland and Portugal advanced (from first and second place in the group, respectively).

Since 2001, during the stressful time of upheavals and changes in our family, I carried extra weight, up to fifteen to twenty pounds. In spurts the excess weight was even twenty-five pounds over the desired level. Stress, a sedentary lifestyle with much driving, little time for walking, and living mostly on a restaurant diet contributed to this situation. My lipid profile was suboptimal, and uric acid came up to 11.6 mg/dl (normal is between 3.5 and 7.2 mg/dl). I had a few bouts of achiness involving small joints of both hands and an area under the left knee (tibial tuberosity). The weight bothered me physically and psychologically in 2003 and 2004, particularly during the trip to the Holy Land, but in 2007 it translated into joint symptoms. I had a few more episodes in 2008 and 2009 and then it stopped. I started taking 150 mg of allopurinol, and the uric acid level came down to around 7 mg/dl (still at the upper limit of normal, but I felt well and did not want to take a higher dose). My weight came down ten pounds, but it was still fifteen pounds over the desired weight.

In addition, plaques of psoriasis appeared on my skin, which were relatively well controlled by the ointments for the time being. (I'd had a few plaques appear on my skin around the age of fourteen or fifteen, but they later disappeared.) There is a connection between psoriasis, elevated uric acid, and extra weight with elevated blood lipids. High glucose (sugar) intake, with the help of insulin, produces fatty acids, which are circulated to other parts of the body and stored as fat (ester of glycerol and three fatty acids), not only in the adipose tissue but also in the liver, which is a crux of the problem. Psoriasis causes increased turnovers of purines, the final product of which is uric acid (from xanthine). Allopurinol inhibits the enzyme converting xanthine to uric acid.

Despite being aware of all of this, I could not practice regular jogging (because of the left knee) which, in combination with reasonable nutrition, could have brought the weight down. Only in 2013 did I commit myself to regular exercise, limiting my driving and sedentary work. After a knee repair in December 2016, I was able to significantly step up the running program.

12.

In 2008 I continued to commute to Fargo to work at the VA, and after the F-150 XLT and the Tiburon were offloaded, a 2008 dark blue metallic Ford Fusion SEL AWD arrived, as well as a 1974 Ford Econoline, which Alek bought for himself and used to practice driving and gain knowledge about the mechanical systems in a car. It was incredibly thirsty for gas, but Alek made only short trips in town. Our third vehicle remained a Ford Edge SE. Ania and Sean had a Ranger and the Elantra in the Twin Cities. Ania briefly had another Volkswagen New Beetle, a dark purple color, but she sold it quickly. In March I traveled to Salt Lake City, as previously mentioned, for a cardiology conference focused on pacemakers and defibrillators. I was not inserting them in Fargo anymore but evaluated patients for possible indications and then consulted the surgery team, if necessary. Making a clinical difference for the patients always brought great satisfaction.

We visited LaCaille restaurant on Wasatch Boulevard in Sandy, Utah, on Saturday evening. I had a bouillabaisse and a glass of red wine, still too sumptuous for the metabolic risk factors I tried to control. On Sunday I went to the Cathedral of the Madeleine for Mass and did not embrace many aspects of the "new" liturgy, which again blurred the distinctions between a priest and the laity. I met in the afternoon for a farewell dinner with our group from Fargo and returned to North Dakota the next day.

I used the YMCA swimming pool while on an assignment in Fargo (sometimes psoriatic plaques were a bit of an embarrassment and a limitation) and went to St. Mary's Cathedral for a Sunday Mass and sometimes during the week. The architecture and the overall liturgical atmosphere provided spiritual support for the time being. I met a Polish-born student and agricultural scientist, Andrzej, and we found many common topics.

The outpatient clinic at Fargo VA was difficult at times because of the constraints imposed on the practicing physicians. There was limited room left for a personal approach. The talks to extend a contract with Fargo VA failed, and in early May we ended the relationship "by mutual agreement." I planned to take a week off in early June to go to Poland to retrace our 1976 high school-era kayak trip in the Masurian Lake District.

Rysiek and I met in Warsaw. We spent the first two days in the capital with his then-wife and stepson. We watched the inaugural soccer game of EURO 2008 in which Poland played quite well but lost to Germany 0:2. The goals were created and scored by two Polish-born players, Miroslav Klose and Lukas Podolski, who had German connections through their families and who had emigrated to Germany as children in the 1980s.

Poland finished fourth in the group with Germany, Croatia, and Austria. Spain won the title, defeating Germany 1:0 in the final.

After the first game loss, we lost interest in the EURO tournament and drove to the region of two thousand lakes. We started near Mrągowo and then reached the village of Krutyń, where the beautiful river Krutynia is at its beginnings. The river is one of the most famous waterways, repeatedly referred to as the most beautiful canoe trail in Europe. It has many bends, and the current is slow. There are beautiful aquatic plants present throughout, such as white water lilies (*Nymphea alba*), yellow water lilies (*Nuphar lutea*), water pineapples (*Stratiotes aloides*) and arrowheads *(Sagittaria sagittifolia)*. The width of the river reaches thirty to forty meters, and the depth is from 2.5 to seven meters. It flows through the municipality of Mikołajki, which is further north and located west of Lake Śniardwy, the largest lake of Masuria and of Poland. Lake Niegocin provides the waterway to Giżycko, where we ended our kayak trip.

In another piece of soccer history trivia, we found out that a noted German coach, Udo Lattek, was born in the tiny village of Bosemb (presently Boże) near Mrągowo. Under the control of the Treaty of Versailles, the East Prussian plebiscite was organized on July 11, 1920, and all 260 inhabitants of the village voted to remain in Germany. In 1945, after World War II, these territories came again under Polish administration. Lattek won all three major European cups in the 1970s with the big teams of Bayern Munich, Borussia Mönchengladbach, and Barcelona, the first coach to do so.

At the beginning of our trip, another double kayak with two tourists from Germany had taken off to the left side of us, and we started a bit of a "competition" with them, traversing the lake heading north. They were a little faster than us over the distance of two kilometers, and we jokingly sighed that "it is always so hard to defeat our neighbors to the west in any competition."

Our trip was thoroughly enjoyable, and Rysiek found the best tourist treasures of Poland to complement our memories from 2003 in Washington DC, Baltimore, Philadelphia, and New York.

We returned to Warsaw in Rysiek's Renault. There was little time left, and I returned to Bismarck via the usual connection of Amsterdam and Minneapolis-St. Paul.

It was providential that an offer from the VA Hospital in Muskogee, Oklahoma, came quickly. I flew each time to Tulsa and then rented a car to drive forty-nine miles southeast to Muskogee. It is interesting to note that the person working at the counter of the car rental company became a Facebook friend and then also a true friend. We met once at Perkins and another time at the Village Inn for dinner and talked about work, faith, and families, Ms. Debra's daughter, and my three children. We are still connected on Facebook. It is heartwarming that sometimes simple, unsullied friendships can happen and make our lives richer.

My place in Muskogee was the Graham-Carroll House, a charming, historic bed & breakfast, which provided a relaxing atmosphere after work and tasty, nutritious breakfasts prepared with care and dedication by the then-manager, Ms. Frances. Physicians and representatives of other professions stayed there for various lengths of time, from one weekend to a few weeks, or even almost a year, such as in my case. I usually stayed in Muskogee for three weeks and went back to Bismarck for one week. With such a steady flow of guests, it was inevitable that sometimes there were differences of opinion on some of the political subjects of the day, but everybody took care to ensure that no ill will persisted after we finished the meal and left the table.

The work in Muskogee was rewarding and interesting. I was busy in the clinic, conducting stress tests, collaborating with echo specialist Dr. Carson Todd, and occasionally venturing to the operating room for a quick consultation or to answer questions and provide advice, mostly about the pacemakers. The nurse practitioner, Ms. Sharon Hanson, was a tremendous influence; a gentle, helpful soul; grounded in her family and in the place of her birth and work. We had a meeting once with a group of cardiologists and internists from the Tulsa and Muskogee area to talk about my possible continuation of work in eastern Oklahoma, but I felt a pull to return to North Dakota to complete what I felt to be unfinished business. I walked a lot in Muskogee in the evenings, finding greater humidity compared to Dakota. There was also more shade from the large trees in our area than in most places in Bismarck. I also discovered the YMCA swimming pool and attempted a strenuous swimming routine for three or four months, the last such effort in this sport in my life.

In April 2009, close to the end of my stay in Muskogee, my parents and Gosia came to visit after I had praised the charm and the atmosphere of Graham-Carroll House many times, and we had a good and warm reunion for the weekend. We upgraded the 2007 Ford Edge SE to a 2008 Ford Edge SEL. We rarely bought a used vehicle, but this one was attractive. It was one year old, with 12,000 miles. It was a dark blue metallic color, with the right combination of power, ride, appearance, and comfort. Alek traded his Ford Econoline for a 1998 Nissan 240X and continued his interest in automotive things.

Also, around that time, I bought a 2009 Ford F-150 STX regular cab in Muskogee. The James Hodge Ford dealership offered good service and support. Two weeks after the purchase, the truck was badly mangled in a parking lot in front of the hospital; almost the entire sheet metal on the left side had to be repaired or replaced. The incident happened inadvertently, of course, and I just had to put everything behind me. I knew then not to be attached to things, particularly vehicles, because they always change. Five years later, in downtown Fargo, I backed into someone's new car's right side while exiting a parking space. It was my blunder this time, also inadvertent, but no doubt stressful for the driver on the receiving end of someone else's error.

In May I went to the Castle of Muskogee to be a part of the Oklahoma Renaissance Festival. It was an afternoon of medieval scenery, costumes, and recreations of the sixteenth-century history of England

and Europe. I saw the street shows of musicians and magicians, watched a jousting tournament, and enjoyed a satisfying meal with an ice cream dessert and soft drink at the end of the day. In June I visited a recent Polish immigrant near Muskogee who restored Bibles. He and his family offered their hospitality, and we had a pleasant afternoon visiting, talking mostly about our current work rather than reminiscing the "old times."

Ania and Sean were married on June 20 at the Church of Christ the King in Minneapolis. She began her study at the University of St. Thomas, which would result in receiving an MA degree in counseling psychology in 2011.

At the end of the month, I returned to Bismarck, but the family bonds were frayed. I felt that Gosia did not want to continue our common journey in marriage; she wanted to distance herself, and the children followed her. She had funds to rent an apartment and be on her own. Alek joined her. Adam finished school at Century High and continued his education at Concordia College in Moorhead, Minnesota. He pursued a law degree and was very active in the Fargo-Moorhead Symphony Orchestra, playing the second violin.

In July I flew to Los Angeles to visit my brother and sister-in-law. California is always great for outdoor sports like walking and running, as well as suntanning and swimming in the ocean at the beach in Oxnard. At the end of the day there was a choice of restaurants or a home-cooked meal. Plate 38 restaurant on Colorado Boulevard in Pasadena became our favorite, and we visited there more often than the other places.

After returning to Bismarck, I applied to MEPCOM (Military Entrance Processing Command) to work at Fargo MEPS (Military Entrance Processing Station). This application moved forward slowly, and I could not count on a regular schedule in the coming months. Hence, I shifted gears and applied for a Locum Tenens internal medicine/cardiology position at the VA Hospital in Hot Springs, South Dakota. This work began in December, around my fiftieth birthday. It was not the happiest time. Family relations were strained and broken, and I had to keep the faith and go forward. I renewed my ties with St. Michael's Church in Mandan and started attending Mass regularly (it was available every other Sunday). The circle of friends replaced my family.

In the meantime, Gosia and Alek left our family home in early November and rented an apartment in Bismarck. Adam was in the Fargo-Moorhead area. Ania was in the Twin Cities. I received a call and business appointment from an entrepreneur, Ms. Judy. We met at Famous Dave's Bar-B-Cue and talked about our work and families in the past. Unfortunately, those times come to an end; we could only reflect on them and carry on. We spent long hours on the phone over the next two years, sharing our problems and talking about business plans for a possible joint venture. It was not meant to be. From 2012 on, our contacts became very sporadic. I visited Judy in Stewartville, Minnesota, in 2016, and we went to Four Daughters Vineyard and Winery in Spring Valley for a meal and glass of their superb wine. I keep her in grateful memory, but our worldviews were different, and we could not mesh our perspectives. There was a generational difference. We exchanged our last message in 2019.

Soon after Gosia's and Alek's departure, I took a long road trip to Detroit, Michigan, to visit Solanus Casey Center in St. Bonaventure Monastery on 1780 Mt. Elliott Street. I decided to take a rental car rather than the truck for convenience reasons. There are 1,120 miles between Bismarck and Detroit, and I rested in Tomah for the night. I managed to briefly visit a distant relative on my mother's side, Gerald Tarka in Calumet City, Illinois, who served as a city treasurer. We exchange Christmas and Easter cards regularly to this day.

I had come to the monastery seeking consolation and spiritual renewal from the life of a gentle Franciscan Capuchin priest, who lived between 1870 and 1957. He was known for his spiritual counseling, gifts of physical healing, and love of violin, a trait he shared with his eponym, St. Francis Solanus (1549–1610), a Spanish Franciscan friar and a missionary to South America, for whom the northernmost mission of California's El Camino Real is named. My Grandfather Karol and son Adam also played violin.

The monastery is an interesting historic place, although adding modern touches in the last years grated on me. I attended Mass at the monastery chapel, and people verbalized their own prayers during a separate evening service. The museum with the details of Fr. Solanus' life, including photographs, artifacts, and written works, is compelling. There is also an opportunity to pay respects to this saintly figure at his simple wooden tomb, already his second resting place after the first exhumation from the Franciscan cemetery in 1987. In November 2017, after his beatification at Ford Field, which I attended, his remains were reinterred in a new black casket with a plexiglass dome to make the casket fully visible but placed in a more exalted and dignified setting. I truly had a feeling of peace after praying to God while at the same time confiding in the Capuchin's power of intercession.

Returning from Detroit, I stopped in St. Louis and spent two days in this historic city, staying at the Marriott St. Louis Grand. I visited the Cathedral Basilica of St. Louis, which is an imposing structure with priceless interior mosaics designed and installed by dozens of artisans. It was built in the early twentieth century as a replacement of the original cathedral, erected along the Mississippi River and now known (since 1961) as the Basilica of St. Louis, King of France, formerly the Cathedral of St. Louis and colloquially as the Old Cathedral. It is near the Gateway Arch, which I visited. I took the tram to the top from where there were superb views of the city to the west and of Cahokia Mounds (pre-Columbian Mississippian culture) on the territory of Illinois to the east.

Soon after returning to Bismarck, I celebrated Thanksgiving in modest circumstances at a hotel with mostly unfamiliar companions at the table and prepared myself for the next chapter. I took off for Hot Springs, South Dakota, on the day of my fiftieth birthday. VA Hospital was surrounded by beautiful, rolling slopes of the Black Hills. The entire region of western South Dakota—between Hot Springs and Custer City, Hill City, Rapid City, Lead, Deadwood, Sturgis, Spearfish, and Belle Fourche—combines the beauty of nature and historic feel. One can almost imagine still being trapped in the period between the Civil War and the Great Depression/World War II.

The company provided lodging at the Flatiron Historic Sandstone Inn in downtown Hot Springs. The town is a southern gateway to the Black Hills and has healing waters and mountain air. The brilliant blue skies and morning smell of pines reminded me of the natural rhythm of life. There were pastry and coffee shops in the neighborhood, an antique mall, and modern restaurants with pizza and American food. The hotel has undergone renovations recently, but even in 2009 and 2010, nothing was lacking to make one feel welcome and comfortable. There was a large TV in the common room with streaming TV services, and I tuned in most often to *Unsolved Mysteries* and *Forensic Files* in the evenings to keep my mind occupied and get ready for sleep.

I found spiritual and social support at St. Anthony of Padua Church with Sunday Mass and the occasional Saturday social event, which consisted of a group of eight to ten men meeting for breakfast with the priest and discussing parish events, family events, and casual current topics.

I met a Polish couple, Wally and Donna, owners and operators of a Budget Host Hotel at the southern outskirts of town, and I visited them for an hour or two almost every weekend. I met their friends, and my social network grew. Even after the conclusion of my work in Hot Springs in April 2010, I visited them twice, in the fall of 2010 and the last time in June 2011, being treated each time as a friend and almost as a family member. With the last visit, I joined in the Crazy Horse Volksmarch, which is an organized hike and a 10K or 6.2-mile woodlands ramble to the world's largest mountain carving in progress. It was good physical exercise and a generally good experience. The slow but steady progress of the monument is impressive.

On February 7, I watched Super Bowl XLIV with a group of friends. It was a good game and a comeback win for the New Orleans Saints over the Indianapolis Colts.

My work, however, did not suit me. I wanted to conclude my involvement in clinical medicine; the other types of work, such as administrative or purely educational, were not forthcoming. This was the last time I interpreted ECGs, echocardiograms, and exercise stress tests, but I was not comfortable dealing with other aspects of work such as prescribing medications. After four months, I felt ready to move on.

While in Hot Springs, I followed some of the events of the 2010 Winter Olympics in Vancouver, from February 12 to 28. The Games were entertaining, with the TV coverage and viewership far exceeding the previous Games in Turin, Italy, in 2006 and in Salt Lake City in 2002. The US team won the most medals overall (thirty-seven); Canada won the most gold medals (fourteen). These were the records up to that point, subsequently bettered by Norway in both categories in the 2018 and 2022 Winter Olympics.

Poland won six medals. Adam Małysz in ski jumping won two silvers (adding to his silver and bronze in Salt Lake City eight years earlier), Justyna Kowalczyk won silver and bronze in cross-country skiing, and the women's speed skating team won a bronze. On February 27, Justyna Kowalczyk won the gold medal in a thirty-kilometer dramatic race, edging out the most decorated cross-country skier in history, Norway's Marit Bjoergen, by 0.3 seconds—the smallest margin of victory at this distance ever. The competition between the two women between 2006 and 2014 was fascinating. Małysz and Kowalczyk finally put Poland on the map in the winter sports category after sporadic successes prior to 2000. Ski jumpers such as Kamil Stoch, Piotr Żyła, and Dawid Kubacki continued to win medals in the last decade, but Kowalczyk did not have successors who matched her achievements. On the other hand, American skiers Kikkan Randall and Jessica Diggins won gold in the team sprint in Pyeongchang in 2018, and the latter won silver and bronze in Beijing in 2022. In addition, both skiers won several World Championship medals and titles.

I returned to Bismarck in early April and started preparing for my next endeavor, finally securing a position of medical evaluator of the military candidates.

The news of a plane crash in Smolensk, Russia, came at that time, in which the president of Poland, his wife, ninety-five top government officials, and the plane crew died. The president's party talked about this event being a planned sabotage or assassination, but in my opinion, the available forensic information points to it being a tragic accident.

Chapter 7

MEDICAL EVALUATION AND ADMINISTRATION

1.

The new phase of my professional life started positively. I went to Fargo for the initial training in May and was assigned work in North Dakota but was also given an opportunity to travel to MEPS stations throughout the United States, which suited me well. Also in May, Alek graduated from high school, and I made sure to go to the graduation ceremonies at Century High. Unfortunately, he was absent, and I had to be content with sending hugs and good wishes in spirit. I went to Sioux Falls, South Dakota, on two or three occasions, and then the radius became even greater with trips to other places that sounded attractive, such as Minneapolis-St. Paul (MEPS is in the historic Fort Snelling), Louisville, Indianapolis, Baltimore, Beckley, West Virginia, Shreveport, Louisiana, Syracuse, Los Angeles, and Jacksonville. The work comprised gathering and categorizing the available information and then making a judgment about the suitability of a candidate for military service. Military applications started from passing the ASVAB (The Armed Services Vocational Aptitude Battery), which measures the candidate's strengths and weaknesses and potential for future success in four domains: verbal, math, science, and spatial. All recruits then complete a medical questionnaire and undergo an evaluation that includes height and weight measurements, hearing and vision exams, urine and blood tests, and blood and alcohol tests. A pregnancy test is required for female recruits, who are examined in a private room with a female attendant and with a drape or gown provided. Physical evaluation is important. Everyone wanting to serve in the military must be in good physical health to endure the challenges of Basic Training and subsequent service. Recruits are asked to perform several exercises to evaluate balance and physical ability, which includes muscle group and joint maneuvers. Then the guidance counselors will help find a job, depending on the ASVAB score and job availability. The Oath of Enlistment ceremony concludes the proceedings.

The traveling work brought satisfaction. There were new personal histories, ambitions, and dreams of young candidates in each place, and the evaluator had to balance accuracy and honesty with the understanding of a person. That is where the waiver system came in, especially for emotional or mental problems that could have happened in a candidate's childhood.

Over the weekend of October 15–17, 2010, Angelus Press hosted its first annual conference in Kansas City, Missouri, on The Defense of Tradition. Before the fortieth anniversary of the founding of Society of St. Pius X, nearly seven hundred people convened at the Hilton Airport Hotel for talks, socializing, and mutual support.

In the fall and winter of 2010/2011, I traveled most often to Baltimore and Beckley, West Virginia. In December 2010, a weeklong trip to Jacksonville, Florida, provided good memories in terms of mild weather, views of the city straddling St. John's River, which empties to the Atlantic Ocean, and the professional effort given. In the spring of 2011, I became familiar with Syracuse MEPS. In June 2011, I spent a week at the Los Angeles MEPS and had a chance to visit with my brother. This time the hotel, which was provided by MEPS, was near the LAX Airport. We had dinner in Pasadena but could not make it to Oxnard in the time allotted.

After returning, the time had come to sell the home in Bismarck and jump into the unknown. Gosia and Alek left Bismarck for Minneapolis, and I rented a motel for two weeks in Bismarck, then for another week in Mandan. A good opportunity came from Syracuse, New York, to work on a steady basis until the rest of the year. The company supplied a comfortable hotel room and a rental car. I returned to Bismarck for a week every month to review mail, which was kept in a post office box. I waited for the time of exit from Bismarck to come naturally.

Just before the closing chapter of life in Bismarck, my former patient and dear friend Andrew Heinle passed away in May. He had a heart condition and had needed surgery ten years earlier. He was a cheerful and caring person. I had the honor to be a pallbearer at his funeral. The burial was with military funeral honors.

2.

In July 2011, Syracuse, New York, beckoned. I landed at the modern Hancock Airport after Independence Day, which fell on a Monday that year, and settled in my new surroundings rather easily. I joined a good and friendly MEPS team. The CMO (Chief Medical Officer) was Dr. Amado Santos, a knowledgeable and kindhearted physician. My continued apprenticeship under him proved a positive and productive experience. I worked Monday through Friday, usually with one or two shorter days, and had weekends off.

I found the historic church of the Blessed Virgin Mary Mother of God on Geddes Street in downtown Syracuse, which served the local SSPX community in that area of the city. A larger building complex operated in Warners, twenty miles northwest of downtown. It housed the priory and academy at that time. Later the church on Geddes Street was put up for sale, and the entire parish life moved to Warners. I felt at home with the liturgy and music. There were processions around the church on special occasions. The priests, including Fr. Stanich and Fr. Post, the first priest ordained for SSPX in the US by Archbishop Lefebvre in 1972, were caring and wise. I met a married couple, James and Eleanor, with whom I have remained friends. A parishioner, Mr. Walter Pidgeon, had heart trouble and unfortunately passed away soon afterwards. He once asked me questions after Mass. I could not help him and did not know a specialist at the Syracuse Heart Institute to discuss the problem with. Hindsight is painful and not always 20/20.

The time went by quickly. I shared my social time on weekends between the MEPS team and the circle of friends in the church, most often visiting Jim and Eleanor. Occasional returns to Bismarck provided a sense of anchoring and continuity. Uncle Lesław died on September 29 in Chorzów, following gastric surgery to remove cancer. On October 7–9, the second Angelus Press Conference in Kansas City, Missouri, on the Kingship of Christ took place, and the following weekend was the twenty-fifth anniversary of my medical school graduation in Columbia, Missouri. Between the events in Kansas City and Columbia, I took time to visit the Solanus Casey Center in Detroit for the second time and then attended the Physicians Alumni Weekend with a class reunion and saw my parents.

Winter came early in Syracuse, with temperatures, winds, and snow precipitation that could easily rival the Dakotas. I frequently had sushi for lunch in October, November, and December, and on New Year's Eve 2011, I experienced terrible abdominal pain in my right lower quadrant, accompanied by nausea and sweats. I dragged myself to the emergency room and had a thorough evaluation with a CT scan to look for appendicitis and, what appeared more likely, a kidney stone. Indeed, a big one was found, later diagnosed as a calcium oxalate composite. I received hydration and intravenous pain medication and went home. Fortunately, I was able to walk to the hotel room and passed the stone ten minutes before welcoming the new year, 2012.

Several lifestyle issues played a role in developing the stone. This was a wakeup call to keep a better diet, lose pounds, exercise more, and always maintain good hydration.

I stayed in Syracuse for two more weeks and flew to Poland to meet with Rysiek. I met with the family in Chorzów first, visiting Uncle Lesław grave. The weather in January was cold, but not as cold as in Syracuse. In Warsaw we made a trip to the Wilanów Palace, built between 1677 and 1696 for King Jan III Sobieski. It survived Poland's partitions (1795–1918) and both world wars, and so serves as one of the most remarkable examples of Baroque architecture in the country. Świątynia Opatrzności Bożej (The Temple of Divine Providence) is six miles to the north, toward the old town and business downtown. It has a modern, forbidding architecture, and despite important ceremonies having occurred there, such as the beatification of Cardinal Wyszyński and Sister Róża Czacka on September 12, 2021, it is not a tourist magnet. We also saw a performance of the play *Sieroty* (Orphans) at the Zygmunt Hübner Theatre, which talked about the problems of family breakdowns, which we both could relate to. We also saw an interesting film, *W Ciemności* (In Darkness) by noted director Agnieszka Holland, which recalled a true story of a Polish sewer inspector in the city of Lwów (now Lviv, Ukraine), Leopold Socha, who used the knowledge of the city's sewage system to shelter a group of Jews from Nazi persecution. In 1978 he was recognized by the State of Israel as Righteous Among the Nations, an honorific given to non-Jews who risked their lives to save Jews during the Holocaust. The film was nominated for Best Foreign Language Film at the eighty-fourth Academy Awards.

I found time to go to Bytom to meet some of my high school friends for a partial reunion. English teacher Ms. Adamek was kind to join our small group, and we had good conversations, especially with Elzbieta (Ela), Barbara, and Roman.

On Sunday, January 22, I attended Mass at the SSPX Church of the Immaculate Conception at Garncarska Street in Warsaw, which I still have contact with through the current availability of Masses and homilies on YouTube.

In the evening I flew back to New York, arriving the same day after time adjustment, and returned to Syracuse by car in the middle of the night extending into the early hours of Monday morning. I finished the assignment in Syracuse on Friday, January 27, and flew back to Bismarck to stay with friends (known from the church in Mandan) until Tuesday, January 31. We went to the theater to see an entertaining film, *War Horse*, directed by Steven Spielberg.

I drove to Fargo on Wednesday, February 1, to start work at MEPS. I had been in contact with Fargo since mid-November, and I accepted the offer to work as a CMO. The first year was supposed to be a trial period, and the future would unfold according to the success of the relationship, or lack thereof. I took my belongings from Bismarck to Fargo in the silver F-150 STX in two trips and put them in storage at U-Haul.

3.

I stayed at a hotel for the first two nights but quickly found a satisfactory apartment near University Drive. The work kept me busy, and I was making headway, but it did not take long to start missing certain aspects of the traveling work. Besides a constant change of scenery, there was less pressure in the latter situation; there was always someone with whom I could consult. Here, a larger portion of the decision rested with the CMO.

I started driving regularly for Sunday Mass to the Chapel in Crookston, Minnesota, seventy-five miles northeast of Fargo. I had a great circle of friends and acquaintances, and I became particularly close with Lanny Baer, his wife Donna, and their children, particularly the five youngest (out of a brood of nine), who were going to SSPX Latin Mass, all very kind, intelligent, and industrious, helping their parents in all aspects of daily life. I befriended Fr. Christopher Darby, and after he left Crookston in December 2012, I visited him periodically in Chicago, assisting him as a driver on his parish mission work in Indiana (in Fort Wayne and Kingsford Heights). I stayed in contact after his move to Kansas City in 2020. In Chicago we had a custom to go to the Staropolska Restaurant on Milwaukee Avenue in the Polish area of the city called Jackowo (from St. Hyacinth Basilica on West Wolfram Street). It served delicious Polish food. We also visited other monumental Polish Cathedral-style churches, generally visible from the Kennedy Expressway, such as Holy Trinity Church on North Noble Street (seen with Rysiek in 2003), St. Mary of the Angels, St. Hedwig's, St. Stanislaus Kostka, and St. John Cantius. However, I attended only Latin Mass at Our Lady Immaculate Chapel on Washington Boulevard in Oak Park or at the priory on Addison Street, sometimes assisting Fr. Darby at his private Mass with the responses.

In July 2012 I made another quick trip to California to visit my brother and sister-in-law. I stayed at Day's Inn Hotel in Camarillo for three nights and briefly watched the highlights of Wimbledon Tennis Tournament. Poland's Agnieszka Radwańska played in the Ladies' Final against Serena Williams. We jogged, swam, and walked on the beach in Oxnard as usual.

The events at Fargo MEPS unfolded quickly. I learned valuable things and hopefully helped the operation for eight months, but in October the time had come to move on. I submitted my resignation on October 12 and felt at peace with this decision.

My state of suspense lasted but a few hours because later the same evening I received a call from a group based in Dallas. CenseoHealth was hiring physician evaluators for the work for Medicare advantage plans. After a prompt credentialling process, I started work on Wednesday, October 17, and set about seeing the plan members, initially in Fargo and then in Grand Forks, Devil's Lake, and Bismarck, all in North Dakota at first. Then a consistent schedule developed to fly to Baton Rouge through Dallas. It was a physically demanding schedule, but interesting and satisfying in all aspects. I stayed most often at Staybridge Suites on Nicholson Street, close to the LSU Campus and LSU Tiger Stadium. It was a comfortable extended stay, residence-type hotel with a great buffet breakfast to start the day and fulfilling dinner on most days to wrap it up. There were numerous restaurants in the neighborhood with the famous variety and taste of Louisiana cuisine on full display. I had eight or nine appointments a day, with a ten to fifteen-minute commute time to reach the next person or couple, and forty-five to fifty minutes to conduct the interview and summary. Some of the places I reached were very remote and required driving on the tertiary roads and creaky wooden bridges around the supremely picturesque Louisiana bayous and woodlands, as well as through cultivated fields. I had the fortune to meet numerous kind and generous people, and, if time permitted, we talked about other topics besides medical. But the medical evaluation was always a primary concern.

From time to time the company chose another hotel, but Staybridge Suites became almost my second home. While in Baton Rouge I attended the SSPX Church of Our Lady of Sorrows (same patroness as in Crookston) on North Sherwood Forest Drive. I found another friendly group of parishioners and an uplifting, reverent liturgy with solid, traditional catechesis.

In early 2013 I decided to approach my own wellness program in a more structured way. I happened upon a gym in Fargo managed by Anytime Fitness in Central Marketplace on 45th Street. There was a friendly group of trainers, and I signed up for a personal training program with Carl Wallin. It was the first time in my life that I had signed up for a comprehensive, versatile muscle training program, including cardio, strength, balance, and flexibility. My weight finally came down twelve or thirteen pounds. I started preparing myself mentally, physically, and financially for left knee arthroscopy, which I felt would be needed within two years or so (it took almost four years, until December 2016, to accomplish it).

In late February there was a mysterious abdication of Benedict XVI with a conclave electing Cardinal Jorge Bergoglio on March 13.

I visited Przemek in July and stayed for three nights at Holiday Inn Port Huenemie. Pirates Restaurant on Victoria Avenue served good burgers, seafood, and cold beer. Unfortunately, it later closed. The Polish men's tennis players did well at Wimbledon that year, reaching semifinals, but Radwańska loss in the semifinal was "disappointing" for casual tennis fans such as myself, especially since Serena Williams lost in the fourth round. Of course, it is about giving your all. "All run, but only one gets the prize" (1 Corinthians 9:24). There are dominant athletes who are a cut above the rest, but in most cases the disposition of the day decides the result.

St. Paul uses the example of earthly athletic pursuits, but he tells us "to go into strict training and run in such a way as to receive the crown that will last forever."

Przemek visited us for Thanksgiving every year between 2010 and 2014. We gathered in the Twin Cities, usually at the Minneapolis-St. Paul Airport Hilton, once at the Courtyard by Marriott Minneapolis West. His wife, Kasia, usually chose to work on Thanksgiving, in order to spend Christmas with her husband. They went to Poland almost every year for Christmas. These gestures by Przemek were very nice. He brought life to our conversations, and we felt like a strong, united family. After Adam moved out of Minnesota to pursue graduate studies in DC, our meetings ceased, but the memories lasted.

The work in Baton Rouge continued throughout 2013 and 2014; in the latter phase, I expanded my work to Shreveport. I suggested several improvements to the work of the evaluators, practicing it on my own at first, to move on from paper documentation to the tablet format with the use of a mobile hotspot out in the field. It was successful 99.9 percent of the time despite the remoteness of the locations. After returning to the hotel, the documentation was saved in a permanent file and transmitted to the company quickly so that the patient information and evaluator payment could be processed faster. Three documentations were lost and reinstated, using the written notes from the field once and repeating the visit on two occasions.

In March 2014 I traded the 2009 F-150 STX for a black F-150 Tremor trim, also regular cab. The silver one from Muskogee tended to develop rust on the left-side bed panel, despite the best efforts of James Hodge Ford to repair it. They helped the situation very well in the fall of 2013, when I drove to Muskogee once for the purpose of a consultation and repair, but the paint peeled after a few months during another harsh Fargo winter when the truck was parked outside.

In May I upgraded my apartment into a newer unit, also on University Drive, a mile south of the previous one. I bought contemporary furniture (a bed, table, and bookshelf) and felt more comfortable.

In June, our parents returned permanently to Kraków, and I was grateful to have a last cordial meeting in Columbia to see them off. Father had some symptoms of a slow heart rate, and I advised him to have a permanent pacemaker. In fact, it could have been done in the spring of 2014. Cardiologists in Columbia knew of the plans to return to Kraków, and it gave everyone a pause. Father received a pacemaker in August, and it made a huge difference in his symptoms. Mother also had irregular heartbeats, and a pacemaker inserted in December helped to regulate them. After saying goodbye to my parents, I visited Barbara and Marshall in Hopkinsville, Kentucky, again after thirteen years. We went for long walks with their dogs to the gym and had a relaxing time.

At the end of 2014, the company extended the opportunity for me to become the regional director, which we discussed with leadership during a pleasant meeting at Dallas Airport in October 2014. After careful consideration, I felt the need to address personal and legal questions regarding the events of January 2007 for which my physical presence in Fargo and full attention of the mind would be needed. Also, I wanted to make a transition to wellness, combining practice with didactics, and the paths were already blazed in Fargo.

In December I attended a 5-day SSPX Ignatian retreat in Phoenix, a difficult but enriching experience. (The second time I went for a three-day retreat in December 2016 in Los Gatos, California).

At the very end of my work in Louisiana, there was a nephrology conference in New Orleans. Father was invited as speaker and sponsor of an annual nephrology award in his name. He flew from Kraków one more time. Mother could not come. Przemek, Ania and her husband, Sean, Adam, and I had a wonderful reunion with him at the Marriott Hotel next to the convention center. I did not share my personal and professional plans at the time.

My relationship with CenseoHealth ended on April 1, 2015.

Chapter 8

WELLNESS AND EDUCATIONAL WORK

1.

The next phase of my life was different from any previous one. It was unhurried, with occasional lectures or meetings on the subjects of physiology of exercise and natural ways of maintaining cardiac health and wellness. I still hoped to restore my relationship with Gosia and the children, broken since 2007, but I realized it would not happen.

I received with gratitude a money gift from my parents, the proceeds from the sale of their house in Columbia. In August 2015 I saw a beautiful white 2014 Dodge Viper at the Corwin Chrysler Dodge Jeep Ram dealership in Fargo. It was displayed as new, with only 394 miles on the odometer. I had been dreaming about driving the Viper since 1990, when it first appeared on the market, and I thought that after a quarter century of waiting, this was my only window of opportunity. The price came down from the manufacturer's suggested retail price of $132,000 to $89,000. I was ready to trade the Tremor, but I also needed to purchase an everyday car, which turned out to be a 2015 dark blue Jeep Renegade from the same dealer. It turned out (after delivery of the car) that the battery in the Viper depleted after such a prolonged stay at the lot, but the dealer took care of it promptly at no extra cost.

I used the Jeep to drive the pastor of Our Lady of Sorrows in Crookston, Fr. Jacques Emily, between Crookston, Browerville, and other destinations such as St. Cloud and Belle Plaine.

In early September 2015, I spent five days in the Greater Los Angeles area. This time I stayed at Przemek and Kasia's condominium in Oxnard for five nights (they worked most of that week). We had a good meeting and dinner with Przemek the night prior to my departure. I spent the last night at the Holiday Inn Express in Port Huenemie so as not to worry about the keys to their condo. The sun, air, and water were rejuvenating to the utmost degree. I enjoyed Hollywood Beach Café near the beach entrance in Oxnard, a good place for a hearty breakfast.

In October 2015 I bought a specialized bicycle at Great Northern Bicycle Company. It remains a good supplement to the overall exercise program.

In December 2015 I flew from Fargo to Denver and then drove to Winter Park for three to four days of skiing. This would be my first visit there since the previous one with Olek and Przemek in April 1988. I rented a Nissan Sentra at Denver Airport and stayed at the Best Western Alpenglo Lodge. Resuming my skiing experience after the ten years since November 2005 in Whistler wasn't too difficult; I still felt reasonably quick and secure on the skis but had the added extra security of using an elastic bandage on my left knee. I repeated the skiing trip in Winter Park in March 2016 (staying at the Alpenglo again).

In late December 2015 I took the Jeep to visit Fr. Darby in Chicago after Christmas, which was celebrated with friends in Glyndon. We went to Crookston for Christmas Mass. Christmas fell on a Friday that year, and I reached Chicago on Saturday evening. I stayed at the Chicago priory for four days and attended daily Mass. We visited the Staropolska Restaurant one evening. On Thursday, New Year's Eve, I took off for Michigan to visit SSPX chapels in Armada (which is a well-worn but noble building, the site of the first SSPX church and seminary in the

United States, established by Archbishop Marcel Lefebvre) and Romeo, a much newer structure, where I welcomed the new year. I stayed at the Super 8 in Flint Township for three nights. From there I drove north and stopped at the Sacred Heart Church in Mancelona, close to Gaylord, which I had visited eight years earlier to meet with the school of echocardiography. I attended Mass in Mancelona on Sunday, January 3 (Alek's birthday), and drove further north to St. Ignace. It was bitterly cold. The Holiday Inn Express was warm and comfortable. The season was not suitable to enjoy Mackinac Island; a look from afar had to suffice. The next morning, I drove to St. Paul via Route 2 on the Upper Peninsula through Iron Mountain and Rhinelander in Wisconsin and then on Route 8 to Stillwater, Minnesota, and St Paul. The distance of 478 miles took nine to ten hours.

I met with Ania and her husband, Sean, at Punch Pizza. I rested for the night at the Holiday Inn in St. Paul and on Tuesday, January 5, I returned to Fargo.

2.

In January 2016 I set aside time to write up my personal and legal inquiry into the events of January 2007. I submitted that I'd received no help—quite the contrary—to try to resolve our family problems. I pointed out incompetence and one-sidedness in assessing the situation by the agencies involved. Unfortunately, Gosia did not want reconciliation, and there was little that could be done. The case went from the district court in North Dakota to the 8th Circuit Court of Appeals in St. Louis, Missouri. I pointed out many physical and legal abuses that had happened. Nobody contradicted me on merit, but instead the statute of limitations clause was used, which is listed at six years for "most actions" in North Dakota. I filed after nine years. My inquiry lasted for over three years with an opinion finally issued in April 2019. The ruling was not in my favor as far as the financial redress requested. A writ of certiorari to the US Supreme Court was not acted upon. I felt morally vindicated and looked to the Scripture verses in Deuteronomy 32:35 and Romans 12:19–21 to conclude this whole saga.

I had already devoted myself to a regular running program since the fall of 2015, which led me to a 10K run in Fargo in May 2016, organized by GoFar Events and led by my acquaintance and business friend Mark Knutson. I achieved the time of 57 minutes and 50 seconds, which is the intermediate level for the fifty-five to sixty age group. (The world record in this age group is 31–32 minutes!) I lowered it to 54 minutes and 58 seconds two years later, in July 2018, but from then on, there was a natural decline. The lists of masters' world records in road running ("masters" means over thirty-five years old) show impressive results of endurance and longevity, with some special eighty-five-year-olds still logging in times well under one hour in a 10K race.

I also had the consolation of enjoying the Dodge Viper on five or six longer trips that year, the favorite destination being Kansas City using Interstate 29. I drove to Kansas City twice in the spring. (I also made a trip to Bondurant Driving School in Phoenix in June, flying from Fargo to Phoenix.) There was a trip to Chicago for a 5K run on July 16, where I met Ann and her two granddaughters. Ann and her husband, Jerry, were one of my first acquaintances in Columbia in October 1983. We enjoyed the run. My time was a pedestrian 28:30, but the knee was giving me sharp twinges of pain. I felt discomfort in it after dinner in a pleasant downtown restaurant and during a long stroll on State Street back to our respective hotels. Stretching, foam rolling, and a good warm-up and cool-down are always important.

Later in July I welcomed Fr. Jacques Emily at the Minneapolis-St. Paul Airport after his return from vacation in France. Father liked the Viper, which took us to Browerville and got me back to Fargo the same evening. Father's warmth and wisdom were always a source of comfort.

In August I flew to Poland for a week to see the family and old friends, Rysiek and Dorota. We attended Mass with Dorota at the SSPX

Immaculate Conception Church in Warsaw, the site of a previous visit with Rysiek in January 2012. I pondered if renewing a friendship with Dorota would be possible, but the developments of the next year gave me a different answer. "No man ever steps in the same river twice, for it's not the same river and he is not the same man" (Heraclitus). Respectful memories remained, and I grieved the death of Dorota's younger son, Piotr, in January 2020, from complications of a rare congenital lung disease. After the Mass I met the priest, Fr. Konstantin Najmowicz, who is continuing his pastoral ministry at the Parish seven years later (overall for twelve years).

I visited my father-in-law and his second wife in Puławy and wanted to visit my brother's wife's family, but we could not make it happen. Instead, we managed a brief meeting with my parents' long-time acquaintance, Maria Starzycka, when she visited them on Smocza Street. She passed away less than a year later from leukemia. We also met with Bożena and her sister Mirka, their mother, Maria, who was uncle Lesław's widow, and Kasia, Bożena's daughter. I did not know their husbands, Dariusz (Darek), Leszek, and Paul (Kasia's American husband), having only met Darek briefly. Sometimes the paths inside the family do not cross, but there must be goodwill and prayer. (I would later meet Leszek at my father's funeral in Kraków in January 2024.) I had visited Aunt Maria's family in Chicago once, around 2010, including her elderly aunt, the recently widowed Ms. Frances Purchla, who was in her nineties at that time. They lived close to O'Hare Airport, and their Polish church nearby was a focal point of religious and social life.

I would fly to Poland again in April 2017, and Przemek's in-laws were kind to come to Kraków this time.

Coincidentally, the seventh Angelus Press Conference took place October 7–9 in Kansas City, with the topic of "The Missions," and the thirtieth Physicians Alumni Weekend took place in Columbia a week later. It was easy to coordinate these two parts of the trip and use the Viper to get to both places.

This was my sixth—and for now my last—personal attendance at the Angelus Conference. The topic in 2012 was "The Papacy"; in 2013 "That She Might Rein"; and in 2014 "The Mass: Heart of the Church." I missed 2015 on "The Family," 2017 on "The Message of Fatima," 2018 on "50 Years Since Humanae Vitae" (Paul VI Encyclical on sensitive subjects related to transmission of human life, promulgated in 1968), and 2019 on "Catholic Marriage." The conference was canceled in 2020; I did not go in 2021 (which took place in December as opposed to the usual date in October and discussed "Catholics and Persecution"), in 2022 on "Restoring All Things in Christ," and in 2023 on "The Catholic Family." Lectures are available on YouTube afterwards.

Arguably even more important events in the life of SSPX, priestly ordinations at the Seminary of St. Thomas Aquinas in Winona, Minnesota, took place in June. I attended the ceremony in 2011, 2014, and 2015. Then, in 2016, the seminary moved to Dillwyn, Virginia. I wanted to go for the consecration and formal opening of the seminary on November 4, 2016 (a week before the Las Vegas 5K run), but the flight from Fargo was canceled because the crew was not available (something to do with the World Series in which the Chicago Cubs won for the first time since 1908 and the ensuing celebrations that altered the schedule of flights through Chicago). I arrived in Dillwyn a day later, on Saturday, November 5, and made the best out of this weekend from every possible standpoint.

The memories from the Alumni Weekend in Columbia were more mixed. There were talks given by graduates that were unnecessary and unfortunate excursions into the world of politics, presenting their subjective point of view. I barely restrained myself from retorting, but at the last minute, as if controlled by some higher power, I bit my tongue, not allowing myself to become involved in bitter polemics. Maybe the reputation that my father enjoyed at the University of Missouri played a role, but I did not want to sully things. Eventually, the true value of every physician's and every politician's work will be judged justly. I had a nice visit with Ann and her husband, Jerry, her daughter, son-in-law, and two granddaughters. We'd just had a meeting in Chicago three months earlier. They looked at the Viper with appreciation for its design and technology. Later in October, I drove to Minneapolis-St. Paul in the Viper and met with Genny and her friends, especially Jan Walter. We used the car for a moment of solitude, reflection, and recollection, praying the Rosary while parked, something that is contrary to the usual understanding of the car's purpose (fast driving).

On November 8, an important presidential election was held.

I flew to Las Vegas the second weekend of November to run a 5K race organized by Humana Rock 'n Roll Running Series. I met Ann and Jerry again. Ann planned to run; her husband was in a supportive role, preferring to walk. I finished 5K on Saturday in 27 minutes and 45 seconds, feeling mild to moderate discomfort in the knee. Ann ran the 5K, too, and then the 10K on Sunday. I attended Mass at SSPX Chapel on Sunday morning. In the evening, we walked with Jerry down the Vegas Strip and admired the runners and the scenery.

I made a trip to Los Gatos, California, for a three-day Ignatian retreat in early December, combining it with skiing in Winter Park afterwards as mentioned previously. The trip in December 2017 remains the last skiing experience thus far in my life. Both in 2016 and in 2017, I stayed at Winter Park Mountain Lodge, a white building on the other (east) side of Route 40 from the ski village. The Mountain Lodge was a bit austere inside but had all the necessities. I had phone conversations with birthday wishes from Genny and Dorota during the 2016 trip within a few minutes of each other while returning from the ski village to the Mountain Lodge and walking on the shoulder of Route 40. Juggling the ski equipment and the cell phone required some dexterity. The knee was ready for an arthroscopy procedure. A left knee arthroscopy was scheduled for Friday, December 23.

3.

Everything went smoothly that day from admission to being wheeled into the operating room and falling asleep under general anesthesia. When I woke up, I felt great psychological relief. Despite the bandages and the postoperative swelling, the left knee felt clean inside, and I had confidence that there would be no more "itching," hesitation, and weakness with weightbearing or limitations of the range of motion. Indeed, the posterior meniscus was resected, the patella cartilage was trimmed and resected (chondroplasty), and everything felt restored. Due to mild posttraumatic arthrosis setting in over the years and losing some of the meniscus cushioning, my knee felt 99.9 percent better instead of 100 percent but with full strength and function.

I went home the same day and slept quite well at night. The next morning, I managed to go the store to buy groceries, but afterwards the knee started hurting and I had to be supine for the next three to four hours. I did not want to take any pain medications except Tylenol. My friend Lanny came in the afternoon and offered me the room in his spacious family house in Glyndon to recover after surgery. This meant the world to me. The emotional support of wonderful people facilitated my healing and overall well-being. I wanted to be a good guest.

Since this was already Christmas Eve, we went to Long Prairie for midnight Mass, with eight people in the large Chevrolet van. My knee was far from comfortable, but I downplayed the symptoms and used crutches to keep up with everybody. Toward the end of the Mass, approaching the Communion rail, I did not want to use the crutches so as not to make too much of a scene, but I thought for a moment that I would fall and cry in pain. I held on to the pews and somehow managed to get back to my place. The crutches helped me to get back to the van, and we were back in Glyndon about 3 a.m. At least we could rest and sleep longer in the morning on Christmas Sunday.

The recovery was quick. I drove home to Fargo on Wednesday

morning and was ready to welcome (quietly) the new year. Dr. Robertson saw me in follow-up in late January 2017, and I started running on February 20. I thought that the surgery would be a miraculous remedy to turn back time and provide me with the legs of a thirty-year-old. I started too aggressively, doing up to eight mile runs in a few days. I came down with Achilles tendinitis in the right leg and had to pause for two weeks. But it did not deter me at all.

The time to sell the Viper had come. The maintenance had been expensive. The tires needed to be replaced, and that would cost at least $3,000. I thought of Sioux Falls as a good place to make inquiries about selling the rare sports car. The market was bigger than in Fargo, and there was something inexplicable that directed me there. I called Billion Auto and talked to one of the sales consultants, who encouraged me to bring the car to show it. I appeared at their parking lot on Friday March 31, 2017. A young, polite, dark-haired man came out and spoke Polish to me. The team looked at the car but told me that "they probably will not be able to offer a sum that would be satisfactory to me." The young man, whose name was Paweł, suggested that I come to visit their family house, in which he lived with his mother, Danuta, and his wife, Daniela. He said that he would sell the car on Craigslist. I was invited after a delicious Polish-style supper to stay overnight in their guest bedroom. I knew that from that moment I would not be able to forget Ms. Danuta.

I returned to Fargo the next day in a rental car and attended Mass in Crookston on Sunday, April 2. Soon I learned from Paweł that he had found a possible buyer in Naperville, Illinois, and had started negotiating.

I traded the Jeep Renegade for a black 2017 Ford F-150 XL, regular cab. I requested a special order, including a four-wheel drive. This truck usually came in a front-wheel drive version. The Jeep was damaged in January by a deer, which had run across the road in Hendrum, Minnesota, during my return trip from Crookston to Fargo. Short winter days with snow and ice on the roads are additional hazards of driving. Corwin Churchill Jeep body shop did an excellent job repairing the front of the car. I managed to dent the back of the car against the lantern at the Eide Ford parking lot just before the transaction. Eide Ford was kind to absorb those costs.

The trip to Poland was in the works for some time, planned between the 11th and 18th of April. Easter Sunday fell on the 16th. We had a pleasant dinner at the "Baran" (Ram) Restaurant in Kraków with our parents and Przemek's in-laws, including his sister-in-law, Ewa, whom I met for the first time. Joanna and Basia were there, too. Knowing that the passage of time is inexorable and equal for all of us, it was good to capture the moments in time. Przemek's father-in-law, Mr. Zbigniew Wawszczak, a very kind gentleman, passed away in 2021 at the age of ninety-one from a chronic heart condition. Two souvenirs from him remain: two volumes of the book *Kresy* (Borderlands), a story of the eastern territories of Poland in 1921–1939; and a Hutsul crucifix hanging at the entrance door in Sioux Falls. Dorota came to Kraków at that time and we met, but there was no real connection between us, and our lives went separate ways according to our respective destinies. I was behaving nervously toward her, not clothing myself in glory.

I attended the Liturgies of the Holy Triduum at the SSPX Chapel of Mary, Mediatrix of All Graces on Zdunów Street.

After returning to Fargo, I drove again to Sioux Falls on Friday, April 28, to celebrate the selling of the Viper. Paweł did an excellent job selling it quickly and at a satisfactory price. We'd asked for $79,000 and received $77,000. We went to Johnny Carino's Restaurant to celebrate. I sat next to Danuta, whom I had started addressing by the diminutive of her name, Danusia.

I returned to Fargo and did not expect that it would take eighteen months, until the end of October 2018, to return to Sioux Falls.

The remainder of 2017 was marked by waiting for the developments in the legal inquiry, participating in occasional street races and other wellness events in Fargo, attending Fr. Solanus Casey's beatification ceremony in Detroit on November 18, and visiting Przemek and Kasia in California for Thanksgiving.

I also gave periodic talks at the gyms about the benefits of running and other forms of workout such as HIIT and strength training. We discussed the physiology of exercise, prevention of injuries, and other practical topics.

We had an excellent time in southern California, with Thanksgiving dinner in Pasadena based on Przemek's provisioning at Whole Foods. The holiday fell on November 23 that year. I went to Anytime Fitness in La Canada on Friday and Saturday, attended Mass at Our Lady of the Angels in Arcadia (as was customary while being in the Los Angeles area on Sundays, sometimes making a special seventy-two-mile trip from Oxnard). La Grande Orange restaurant in Pasadena offered a great lunch after the Mass; later I went to Oxnard to relax and exercise.

The whole week in Oxnard went fast. I honed my endurance and speed while running daily. Przemek came on Friday and stayed until my departure on Saturday, December 2, when I flew to Denver.

On Sunday, December 3, I attended Mass at St. Isidore Church in Watkins, sixteen miles east of Denver. While in Denver, I stayed at the DoubleTree Hotel in Aurora each time in 2015, 2016, and 2017. From there I went to Winter Park and skied until Friday, December 8. There was a noticeable difference in the feel and performance of the knee compared to the previous December. I left the slopes in the morning, wanting to be in Watkins again for the evening Mass, since this day is an important Catholic feast celebrating Mary. Everything was very much in place. I flew back to Fargo on Saturday, ready to go to Crookston on Sunday.

4.

Christmas 2017 and New Year 2018 came quickly. I called Danuta from time to time and we exchanged wishes, but our social ties did not go beyond that.

The year 2018 turned out to be quite eventful. I was preparing for the Sanford Fargo Marathon, scheduled for Saturday, May 19. I ran diligently in the spring, eighty miles per month, with the longest single run of twenty miles. I ran five to six shorter "competitive" races, usually organized by GoFar Events. The marathon itself was a memorable event. My goal was to achieve the time of 4 hours and 10 minutes, and for that one needs to progress at 9:33 minutes per mile or 5:55 minutes per kilometer. I followed the pacemaker runner with a big 9:30 sign. It went well for twenty miles, but after that I experienced severe muscle fatigue and tightening and could keep the pace of only 11:15 minutes per mile over the last 6.2 miles (ten kilometers). My overall time was 4:29:15 minutes. I regretted casual chat with my fellow runners during the first half of the race, which, albeit brief, could have exhausted energy reserves faster. I kept good hydration and carbohydrate feeding during the race. Marathon running demands full respect and complete mental and physical preparation. The left knee felt great. The calorie count stood at 3,840 kcal burned. I had a nutritious meatloaf dinner at the Granite City Restaurant afterwards, so the overall weight loss was not significant.

I was ready to resume six- to eight-mile daily runs in two or three days. Also at that time, I campaigned for a seat on the Fargo School Board, without success, but I was glad that my legal questions addressed from Fargo to Bismarck were duly publicized in the newspaper. It provided a measure of satisfaction.

The World Cup in Russia took place from June 14 to July 15. The US missed qualifying. Poland finished at the bottom of Group H after two quick losses to Senegal and Colombia; the latter team advanced along with Japan (Poland's win against Japan in the last game was again meaningless). The German team, World Champions in 2014, finished the bottom of their group in 2018, which had never happened in the history of the previous eighteen World Cup campaigns since 1934. Germany always reached at least a quarterfinal, and had reached a semifinal thirteen times, which is the most of all national teams. Only

Brazil has more titles (five) than Germany (four). Italy also has four titles, but two of them are very remote, in the 1930s. Brazil and Italy have less places in the last four than Germany (eleven and eight).

5.

In June I called Danuta after dinner at a Radisson Hotel restaurant in Fargo. I'd had four or five glasses of wine, and my emotions toward her spilled over. I was too brash and profusely apologized on a postcard the next day. I refrained from all conversations for almost four months.

In the meantime, I flew to Chicago for a Rock 'n Roll half-marathon scheduled for Sunday, July 22 at 7 a.m. I wanted to stay at one of the downtown hotels, but because of very unfortunate planning, I had to ask Fr. Darby for hospitality at the priory. Father was always kind and bailed me out. I finished with the time of 2:08:43, good for 3,446th place out of 8,991 runners. The average time was 2:20:00.

I drove to Our Lady Immaculate Church in Oak Park immediately after the run and entered the building two minutes before the start of a 10 a.m. Mass. Unfortunately, a quick wash and a change of clothes were needed, so I was seven or eight minutes late in the pew. The remainder of the Sunday was pleasant, and I ended up going to the Old Warsaw restaurant on Harlem Avenue. Unfortunately, the restaurant was in the process of being closed permanently, so I could not order food. I gladly drove to Staropolska.

The intense running during the entire year 2018 took its toll on me. I started feeling muscle aches and had a few areas of skin redness, likely related to psoriasis. In September I came down with extensive shingles on my right arm and armpit, and from that point on I turned my running down a notch. August was the last month in which I logged eighty-four to eighty-five miles a month. Afterwards, forty miles a month became the norm.

I visited Adam in Washington DC on August 17–20 and stayed

at the Inn of Rosslyn, which Adam had reserved beforehand. It was a thoroughly enjoyable weekend. I experienced the nation's capital from a different perspective than in 1985 and 2003. Every day started with a morning jog near the Arlington Cemetery and Iwo Jima Memorial. I went to Sunday indult Latin Mass (not SSPX) at Saint Mary Mother of God Catholic Church on 5th St. NW. The liturgy was reverent, the same as in SSPX, but I sensed more modern themes or references in the sermon. We had dinner and pleasant conversation at Barley Mac restaurant in Arlington on Saturday and at a Thai restaurant near the church on Sunday. I flew back to Fargo on Monday.

On September 7, Ania gave birth to a healthy boy, my first grandson. August Joseph (Gus or Gucio) brought immense joy to the family; I always think of him and pray for his and his parents' spiritual and physical wellbeing.

The following week Przemek visited me in Fargo. He gave a lecture on the newest oncology medications used in the treatment of neoplasms of the genitourinary tract. Afterwards we had a glass of wine and dessert at the Delta Marriott Hotel. We talked about our parents' upcoming sixtieth wedding anniversary on October 11. Przemek was going to fly to Kraków with Kasia. I had to cancel my travel plans, which also included a high-school class reunion. I accepted fate's intervention in the form of shingles and other indispositions without distress.

On October 9, Danuta called me and said she forgave me for my June impudence and that we could talk and visit. Of course, I was overwhelmed by emotions. I knew that Danuta is a very special person and we have many things in common. I drove to Sioux Falls on Monday, October 29, and stayed until Thursday, November 1, All Saints Day, driving all the way to Crookston for a 2 p.m. Mass. I returned three weeks later, on Thanksgiving Day. We spent the holiday with Danusia's Polish friends, Tomasz, who is a physician, and his wife, Ola, in Hendricks, Minnesota. Their young boys, Matthew and Luke, were very happy and well-behaved. Returning to Sioux Falls we became lost in the countryside and got home after 1 a.m. We had a rental car, and the cell phone GPS didn't work due to a weak signal in the "wilderness."

On November 4, I saw Ania and baby Gus at the Mall of America in Bloomington, Minnesota. It was a beautiful occasion. Somehow, after 2011, we always chose to meet out on the town rather than at their home.

In mid-November, I went through another misfortune with the black F-150 XL, having been on the receiving end of a careless driver's ramming the entire right side of the truck (as opposed to the left side of the silver truck nine years earlier in Muskogee). The accident happened in Fargo in wintry weather. The repair took three weeks, and I used a rental car during that time.

In December Danusia and I met in Sioux Falls on December 21–22, shortly after my birthday and just before Christmas, but we celebrated the holidays separately. I also met with Lanny's brother, Mr. Donovan Baer, and his family in Sioux Falls. They offered me hospitality at their home for one night. We had dinner at Red Lobster while Danusia visited T.J.Maxx and the Empire Mall nearby. I drove to Sioux Falls again for the second weekend of January 2019, and this time we shopped together at Marshall's and T.J.Maxx.

In early January 2019 I formalized the longstanding state of separation from Gosia in Fargo Court. A decree of divorce was granted per my request.

There was a three-month break in my contact with Danusia, but we talked on the phone frequently. Paweł decided to fly to Poland on February 14, and on March 14, Danusia received the tragic news of his passing. This happened while we had a conversation on Skype. Danusia asked me to come to Sioux Falls to help her. I drove to Sioux Falls through a snowstorm with complete whiteout conditions the very same day (Thursday), and I ended up being stuck with the truck in deep snow on the shoulder. My speed was 5 mph, but I lost the sense of positioning on the road. A providential couple took me to Sioux Falls in their passenger vehicle, and the next day Danusia and I drove to

Chicago in her 2008 Chevrolet Malibu. The weather was better. We met at her acquaintances' house. Danusia's older son Piotr came (Chicago is his base; he drives the truck), and they went to the airport to fly to Warsaw. I said goodbye and set off for Fargo. It was already late in the evening, and I managed to get to Pewaukee, Wisconsin, where I stayed at the Holiday Inn Express. We had one more emotional conversation before her departure. I fell asleep shortly thereafter.

I returned to Fargo the next day, but not before running out of gas at one point in Wisconsin. I was unfamiliar with the gauges of the Malibu and planned poorly. A Good Samaritan (a lady with another female companion in her car) gave me a hitch to the nearest gas station, which was two miles away, along with twenty dollars to buy a canister and two or three gallons of gas. People's generosity can be very moving. The canister is still in our garage.

The next day, Sunday March 17, Lanny and his daughter Celine followed me back to my truck in South Dakota, south of Summit, north of Watertown. Lanny pulled the F-150 out of the shoulder with his Silverado. I used Danusia's Malibu in Fargo for the next two weeks, serviced it, and set off for Chicago on Friday, March 29. We met Ania, Sean, and Gus at a bakery and café in Minneapolis. Gus was already six months old and was growing fast. I went to Mass at SSPX Chapel in St. Paul on Sunday and reached Chicago in the evening, staying at the Spring Hill Suites Hotel. On Monday, April 1, Danusia's plane from Warsaw was delayed more than five hours. I bided my time at Staropolska and the Polish bookstore, Quo Vadis. She finally landed at 8 p.m., and we started our journey back to Sioux Falls, stopping at Rich's Delicatessen just before they closed at 10 p.m. and stocking up on a variety of Polish foods.

We rested for the remainder of the night in Onalaska, Wisconsin, going to sleep after 2 a.m. We got up reasonably early to visit the Shrine of Our Lady of Guadalupe. The church and the surroundings were beautiful. Danusia found much peace after the terrible events of the previous weeks, and I also found this place to be very consoling. We spent three hours there and made it to Sioux Falls late in the evening.

For the remainder of 2019 I established a regular schedule of being in Sioux Falls every weekend starting April 12. I had worked for the supplemental insurance company Aflac since October 2018 (and concluded my involvement in November 2019). Weekends were busy with yard work. I enjoyed Saturday dinner before going back to Fargo (and Crookston) on Sunday morning. On June 16, there was a dense fog in the morning, and I could not drive three hundred miles that day. Danusia was very much in agreement. We went to the church of St. Therese of Lisieux and established spiritual counseling with the pastor of the parish, Fr. Kevin O'Dell. I requested a canonical opinion from the marriage tribunal in Sioux Falls about my marriage contracted in 1985. I initiated the inquiry on August 1. (I attempted to initiate the process with SSPX in November 2018, but the circumstances were not favorable to proceed with it at that time).

We went to Lake Okoboji in northern Iowa on four occasions (three times combining Saturday and Sunday and once on Saturday only) in August and September, seeing the Shrine of the Grotto of the Redemption in West Bend, Iowa, on our first trip. We went to St. Joseph Catholic Church in Milford, Iowa, twice, and otherwise used as much time as possible to soak up the sun in the touristy area of Arnolds Park and West Okoboji on the beaches around the beautiful lake. We finished the day each time in the Okoboji Store restaurant, which has a great waterfront location with marina views, and offers hearty pub grub and cold beer. Each trip to Okoboji was immensely rewarding, even though we did not have water toys and many comforts. We visited shops, used walking trails, enjoyed local restaurants and ice cream venues, and listened to a conference of the environmentalists and marine biologists in an outdoor setting under a large tent in Arnolds Park.

I stayed in Sioux Falls between Thanksgiving and December 8, and I used this time to visit the marriage tribunal and enroll in the MBA

Program at the University of Sioux Falls. Fr. O'Dell told us about a Latin Mass community in Salem, South Dakota (forty-three miles west of Sioux Falls), but Danusia didn't express interest, and I made a concession, staying reluctantly with the English-language liturgy in the churches in Sioux Falls for the time being.

The momentous year 2020 began. I started classes in early January for the course in organizational dynamics but prepared a trip to Chicago to renew my Polish passport. Danusia agreed to join me. We accomplished our journey (in a rented Nissan Rogue) on February 22–24 and stayed at the Ambassador Hotel by Hyatt near Lake Michigan, close to the Polish consulate on N. Lake Shore Drive. It was unusually warm. We visited the historic Polish churches (Holy Trinity, Stanislaus Kostka, John Cantius, and St. Hyacinth, as we did with Rysiek and Fr. Darby before) and went to Latin Mass in Oak Park. While at the Staropolska restaurant, where Piotr joined us for dinner, I received a call from Jan Walter who said that Genny had died in her native Kenya after a fall. She was doing missionary work after leaving Minnesota in 2018. I felt great sadness, which was allayed by prayer and hope over time.

Throughout our entire trip I had a general sense of foreboding, knowing that this was an election year. It was just "too quiet to be true."

And indeed, the official announcement of the new public health crisis struck in March. There were restrictions, lockdowns in many places in the world, mandates, and changes in travel and school schedules. Classes changed from in-person to remote on Zoom. In Sioux Falls, the encumbrances to daily routine were relatively small, although masks in classrooms were one obvious noticeable difference.

Danusia and I agreed on my permanent move from Fargo to Sioux Falls. I sold or donated my belongings to a charitable company, and the rest we took in two runs in the truck during the first days of May. Soon thereafter I received a letter from the marriage tribunal in Sioux Falls saying that there were reasons to consider our 1985 marriage as "not fulfilling the matter of Catholic Sacrament" (mutual consent of the couple to live together as spouses in a lifelong union), therefore paving the way to an annulment. Gosia (probably with other members of the family) appealed this decision, and it would take three more years for it to be confirmed by Roman Rota, the highest appellate tribunal in the Catholic Church. These considerations touch the deepest layers of the human soul, conscience, mind, and heart. I have much respect for Gosia. I believe in marriage and see many lifelong unions around. I wish it for my children, grandchildren, and look forward to what the Providence has in store for me.

I proceeded with the MBA program. Danusia and I could not go to Okoboji in the summer. The Tokyo Olympics were postponed until 2021, as well as EURO 2020. There was a ripple effect in the calendar with the IAAF World Championships in Athletics scheduled in Eugene, Oregon, for 2021 being moved to 2022. The FIFA World Cup went on in Qatar in December 2022. The Beijing Winter Olympics took place in February 2022. There were "closed bubbles" created for the athletes, staff, and journalists, with smaller live audiences, more in the earlier events in Tokyo and Beijing, less so in Oregon or Qatar. Many world and Olympic records were set.

In June 2020 I traded the 2017 Ford F-150 XL for a silver 2020 Ford F-150 XLT crew cab. Danusia's son Piotr gave me the "incentive" by buying a BMW sports car, so I again fell for "something new." It was comfortable and served us well on the long-distance trips. In November 2020 there was an unusual and charged presidential election.

In April 2021, Ania and Sean welcomed their second child, Nora June, a very pretty, cheerful girl, my first granddaughter. I offer daily prayers for her, as for her brother Gus.

I graduated on May 16 with a GPA of 3.9 and the MBA Excellence Award. Danusia went to Poland three days later to see her elderly mother and the rest of her family. We drove to Chicago in our F-150. I stayed at Westin O'Hare for the night. Danusia returned on June 12, and we stayed for one night at Sheraton Suites.

We went to Okoboji once in August, only one Saturday. Okoboji Store was as welcoming as ever. In June 2021 I changed my parish from St. Therese to Our Lady of Guadalupe, where I stayed until November 2022. (I relied for a while on YouTube streaming of a Latin Mass until May 2023 when Lanny told me of St. Dominic's Church in Canton, South Dakota). His family had a reunion at Newton Hills State Park nearby, which I was privileged to join for the afternoon. The priest and Latin Mass community had moved from Salem to Canton not long before.

Danusia and I drove to Kansas City over the Independence Day holiday in 2021 and stayed at the Hilton Airport Hotel. We went to Lake Jacomo near Blue Springs to enjoy water, sun, and nature. In the afternoon we drove to the downtown Plaza to Buca di Beppo restaurant. On Sunday morning we went to SSPX St. Vincent's Church. The rest of Sunday afternoon was devoted to visiting sports stores to look at clothing and going back to the lake. We had late dinner at a Mexican-style restaurant in Blue Springs. The return to Sioux Falls went smoothly on Monday with a stop at the Olive Garden restaurant in Omaha.

A week after the Labor Day weekend, Danusia and I visited Tomasz and Ola and their sons in Chicago. We had a nice time with plenty of walking, jogging, restaurant visits, and attending Mass on Sunday (I took a longer drive to my familiar SSPX Church), spending time at home, playing table tennis in the (yet unfinished) basement, and watching movies.

Danusia's mother passed away in late September. Sadly, it was not possible for her to fly to Poland at that time.

Throughout that time, I searched for administrative or didactic jobs related to health and wellness or career mentorship. One such opportunity came in September 2021 to work for Nepris, Inc. (which later became Pathful, Inc.), which comprised volunteer work to aid educators in supporting students' career readiness as an industry professional. I reached out to the classrooms throughout the country via Zoom, slowing down my involvement in May 2023. I studied French, Spanish, and Russian on Duolingo since 2020 to acquire some conversational ability in these languages.

On November 20, Danusia and I took off from Sioux Falls to visit Przemek and Kasia in Pasadena and Oxnard (my ninth trip in twenty-two years, Danusia's first). We spent time exclusively in Oxnard; their house in Pasadena was undergoing extensive remodeling. The trip took us only two days going west. The first day we covered 920 miles, stopping at 1 a.m. in Clifton, Colorado, close to the border of Utah. We took very brief breaks to eat homemade sandwiches for lunch and to buy gas once. The second day (Sunday) we reached Oxnard at 10 p.m., having driven 830 miles, tuning into the Latin Mass on YouTube during a brief stop.

Our Thanksgiving dinner was excellent at the Waterside restaurant. We also had dinners at Raven's Tavern, SeaFresh, and Moqueca Brazilian Restaurant at Channel Islands Harbor. Danusia and I visited two of the twenty-one famed California missions, San Buenaventura and Santa Barbara. Przemek and I used his kayak for a picturesque, physically and visually rewarding ride around the Channel Islands Harbor. I jogged two or three miles every morning, and we appreciated every minute of the sun and every drawing of a breath on the beach. Przemek was with us the entire Thanksgiving weekend, November 25–28. Kasia, unfortunately, was on duty at the hospital.

Danusia and I went to Mass at Our Lady of the Angels in Arcadia on Sunday morning. We stopped for lunch at Plate 38 restaurant in Pasadena, briefly visited historic St. Andrew's Church, and drove back to Oxnard on Route 1 along the Pacific coastline. We saw the impressive SoFi Stadium, home to the Rams and Chargers NFL teams, and Kia Forum (formerly The Great Western Forum) to our left (west) while northbound in Inglewood. Unfortunately, by the time we reached Santa Monica, the sun had already set, and we did not see the ocean well. After getting home, we relaxed and talked with Przemek for the rest of the evening. He stayed in Oxnard for the night before leaving for work at St. John's Hospital in Santa Monica the next morning. Our stay in Oxnard lasted until Friday, December 3, and we took three days to return, the first night stopping in Las Vegas for a brief walk on the Strip and the second night in Denver, reaching Sioux Falls on Sunday evening. It was much colder than in California and Nevada.

In 2022 I continued my running and wellness program and made contacts with the University of South Dakota OLLI (Osher Lifelong Learning Institute) to participate in periodic educational events, speaking on subjects related to health, wellness, and exercise physiology from a broader historical and cultural perspective.

In January and February 2022, while practicing for a 10K run in Sioux Falls, I logged 115 and 102 miles under the guidance of a Garmin Virtual Coach. This was done, however, mostly on a treadmill in the gym, being more protected. On March 12, 2022, I achieved 60:18 minutes in the "official" race, running outside in the temperature of only 28°F.

In late February 2022, a conflict between Russia and Ukraine erupted. A month later we again drove to Chicago in the F-150 XLT, this time to renew Danusia's Polish passport. We stayed at the same Ambassador Hotel. The proceedings at the consulate were smooth, but Danusia said that she only had a standing option inside with new cubicles and sequestrations installed since 2020. The companions were not allowed inside at all.

In July I went to Kraków for a week. Przemek and his wife were in Kraków at the same time, and we had good family meetings. We went to the Galeria Kazimierz (a large, modern shopping center) and the Dr. J. H. Jordan Park. We visited with Joanna, Basia, and Karolina. It was good to see our parents strong and cheerful despite their advancing years. In August I traded the F-150 XLT into a silver 2022 Ford Bronco Sport. I used it three times to drive to St. Paul, in October (by myself) to see Ania, Gus, and Nora at the Sitzer Park in Shoreview; on New Year's Eve to see them again with Sean at Pizza Luce in Roseville and then to unwind at a Buck Hill ski resort in Burnsville with Danusia, who was with me all the time; and for the third time in April for Easter (by myself). I attended the Easter Vigil Liturgy at the Chapel of the Immaculate Heart of Mary in Oak Grove. The Ford Bronco took me three times to Kansas City, first to meet with Fr. Darby in November 2022. We attended religious events but also had a very pleasant time at Buca di Beppo at the Plaza. I drove again on March 18 to visit the priory, only to be stricken with the news that Fr. Darby had died suddenly the night before. I went back to Sioux Falls but came back for the funeral Mass on Thursday.

Danusia was studying for her American citizenship exam in 2022 and completed the course successfully. She had to postpone her exam, scheduled for September, because of a dental problem, which just happened at an inopportune time. She passed everything very well in late October. The swearing-in ceremony, scheduled for mid-December, had to be postponed until late in January 2023 because of harsh weather conditions throughout the winter.

The FIFA World Cup took place in Qatar in December. The Poland and US teams advanced from their groups into the first knockout stage (1/8 final), losing to France and the Netherlands, respectively. Poland had a world-class player in Robert Lewandowski, who was in much better form than in 2018, but the team could not be successful against Argentina and France, the eventual finalists, in the last game of group play and in the Round of 16, respectively. Lionel Messi confirmed his status as probably the best player in history. (The memories of Poland defeating Argentina in 1974 and France in 1982 in the previous World Cups must suffice. Grzegorz Lato provided unique inspiration at that time).

Super Bowl LVII was played in Phoenix on February 12. It was an entertaining spectacle, and, with my KC ties, I was happy with the result. I was always appreciative of athletic achievements, and it was no different with Patrick Mahomes, Harrison Butker, and Jalen Hurts.

Butker's attachment to Latin Mass is an interesting side story.

After increased traveling activity in March and April, I continued it in early May with my last trip to Saint Mary's on May 2–4 to attend the consecration ceremony of the new Church of the Immaculata. I visited Father Darby's grave next to the church at Our Lady of Peace Cemetery. The drive on the secondary roads in Kansas and Nebraska was relaxing, with picturesque towns, rivers, fields, and quaint, excellently maintained roadside churches, such as Saint Columbkille in Blaine, Kansas. Only in Omaha, I rejoined I-29 to return home to Sioux Falls.

Chapter 9

CONCLUSION

1.

The story concludes in May 2023 for now, but it will continue according to destiny written for all of us. I hope to nourish and improve our family contacts. I want my children and grandchildren to be strong and prosper. Mother will turn ninety in a month; Father would reach ninety in twelve months. They will celebrate sixty-five years of their marriage. Gosia's father is almost ninety-three. Przemek is sixty. Longevity is to be appreciated.

I took the year of 1903 as a symbolic beginning of my reflection; it was the year when Pope Pius X began his pontificate. He described modernism as a "synthesis (sewer) of all heresies" and took the steps to combat it. Modernism was a movement very active in 1890–1910 that sought to reinterpret traditional Catholic teaching in light of nineteenth-century philosophical, historical, and psychological theories, and called for freedom of conscience (detached from the source of conscience). It was suppressed but returned in the 1950s around the time when the Second Vatican Council was convened. The prophetic events and messages in Fatima, Portugal, in 1917 are serious. World

War II happened as predicted, and it was a terrible chastisement. The Third Secret was supposed to be revealed in 1960; it was officially revealed in 2000, but questions remain about the veracity of the official version of making John Paul II the central figure of it. The Third Secret spoke of the great loss of faith (apostasy), which would begin at the very highest levels of the Church. Altering the dogma and the liturgy would threaten the life of the Church, the world, and individual souls. There is consolation in the words of Our Lady that these events are not irreversible, that the future is conditional on our involvement, that the acts of penance and trust (consecration of Russia by the Pope) have power to divert calamities. The Rosary is a powerful weapon. Mary says that her Immaculate Heart will triumph, and an era of peace will be given to the world. These words were authenticated by a great Miracle of the Sun in Fatima on October 13, 1917.

We now live in the time of great dangers, big upheaval, attempted Great Reset, Fourth Industrial revolution, New World Order, global government, and hostile international relations. These are the results of "spreading the errors of Russia" and advancement of Communism throughout the world. We must continue our cultural, philosophical, and political conversation in a civil but clear tone. We need to properly read the unfolding signs.

While we cannot be certain of what the future has in store for each one of us, I hope we can meet again in the next five to six years to read the second volume of this book under circumstances that are more favorable to us, our families, friends, work teams, societies, and the world.

The End

NOTES

The names of the countries in the events of the 1960s, 1970s, and 1980s are stated as they were known at that time.

Czechoslovakia existed as a Marxist-Leninist single party socialist republic from 1948 to 1989, and as a federal parliamentary republic until 1992. In December 1992, it peacefully split into two sovereign states of the Czech Republic (recently often called Czechia) and Slovakia.

Yugoslavia ("Land of South Slavs") existed between 1918 and 1941 as the hereditary kingdom, and from 1945 to 1992 as a federal republic. It disintegrated in April 1992 into the successor states of (currently) Serbia, Montenegro, Slovenia, Croatia, Bosnia and Herzegovina, North Macedonia, and Kosovo.

German Democratic Republic, colloquially known as East Germany, was created on October 7, 1949, from the Soviet-occupied zone in World War II. Federal Republic of Germany, colloquially known as West Germany, was created on May 23, 1949, from the states formed in the three allied zones of occupation held by the United States, the United Kingdom, and France. The city of Berlin was also divided. Almost a year after the fall of the Berlin Wall on November 9, 1989, The Treaty on the Final Settlement with Respect to Germany, also called the Two Plus Four Agreement, was signed in Moscow, USSR, on September 12, 1990. The final reunification happened on October 3, 1990.

The Soviet Union, officially the Union of Soviet Socialist Republics (USSR), was a transcontinental country spanning northern Eurasia that existed from December 30, 1922, to December 25, 1991. It was succeeded by fifteen independent states: Russia, Belarus, Ukraine, Kazakhstan, Turkmenistan, Azerbaijan, Armenia, Tajikistan, Uzbekistan, Kyrgyzstan, Georgia, Moldova, Latvia, Estonia, and Lithuania.

The proper name of the European country on the North Sea coastline is the Netherlands. The informal name in Dutch and English is Holland, but only two provinces—North Holland where the capital Amsterdam is located and South Holland with The Hague, the country's administrative center—are properly so called.

Hutsuls are an East Slavic ethnic group spanning the parts of Western Ukraine and Romania.

There are three relatives with the name of Barbara: in Kraków (diminutive Basia is frequently applied), in Edinburgh (who usually goes by her full name), and in Hopkinsville, Kentucky (diminutive Basia is sometimes applied).

With Nephrology Around the World, an autobiography by my father, Zbylut J. Twardowski, served as a reference for some of the details from the early years in Poland.

www.ingramcontent.com/pod-product-compliance
Lightning Source LLC
Chambersburg PA
CBHW070350090426
42733CB00009B/1354